THE ECONOMICS OF THE INVISIBLE GLOBAL GOOD-GOVERNANCE GOVERNMENT (G^4) AND THE AID-DEPENDENT ECONOMY

BY

TESHOME MULAT

Table of Contents

List of Boxes

List of Tables

List of Figures

Preface

There are dramatic developments taking place in the world today. On the one hand, mind-boggling changes are occurring, which are tearing societies apart, causing massive destruction of economy and society by torrential rains and flooding and volcanic eruption, drought and starvation, uncontrollable rage, conflict and terrorism, as well as world monetary crises and global economy meltdown. On the other hand, there is also that creativity and problem solving capacity in man which is being reflected by the cooperation, indeed increasing cooperation, among governments to regulate nature and control human destructiveness. It is this cooperation among governments that in this monograph we call the *invisible global good-governance government* (G^4). "Invisibility" is self-evident, because G^4 has not reared its head fully yet, it shows its presence by certain manifestations of its existence. Global good-governance government can be likened to an idea, a manmade religion of sorts, which manifests itself in the G-8, G-20, UN Security Council, the UN General Assembly, the NATO-Russia meeting, the WTO, The China-USA summit, the Russia-China Summit, etc.

It also manifests itself as an organization or a system of governance when it bombs the Afghan Taliban, dismantles the Balkans. delivers food aid to the starving population in the Horn of Africa area, organizes and mans ships from many nations off the coast of Somalia to combat piracy, pays for UN forces to keep peace in the Congo and Sudan, declares universal human rights and protection, establishes the UN Millennium Development Goals, threatens to book and bring to justice African dictators for genocide and crimes against humanity, and holds negotiations with the governments of Iran and North Korea so that they give up their nuclear bomb building ambitions.

However, in spite of its invisibility, much hope is pinned down by humans everywhere on the invisible global good-governance government (G^4) to solve all outstanding problems, be they natural or manmade, which mankind is confronted with today.

If many study groups about the bottom billion residents of the "dangerous cesspool" (to use Prof. Collier's identification) are not dwelling much on the nature and significance of G^4, it is not because they failed to realize that the fate of the residents of the cesspool is in the hands of G^4. In fact Collier and the group take that for granted: G^4 must take the responsibility to extricate the billion souls from the morass of perpetual poverty and underdevelopment in which they find themselves. One of the instruments being applied to do the job has traditionally been "aid".

However, in trying to save the cesspool residents through aid, and this is where the Collier group are making a contribution, G^4 or any other benefactor must take into account that all aid is not necessarily beneficial to the aid recipient. In the study, *The Bottom Billion*, (Collier, 2007) concluded, "…aid was not very effective at raising growth in the conditions of poor governance and policies that typified the bottom billion" (p. 105). Ex ante conditionality aid (i.e. aid acquired on the basis of promises to reform) was wasteful and ineffective, and ex post conditionality aid (or aid based on actual performance of reform) caused aid inaccessibility to the bottom billion. Technical aid for non-reforming failed-economies is useless and could even be crowding out local skills, while it becomes a potent weapon for economic growth in reforming economies on the turnaround. Project aid under the control of the aid-giver could achieve plan targets but may eventually turn out to be a waste in view of loss of momentum and lack of project interconnectedness and growth dynamics. Thus, one can make a borehole and provide piped water to the community. But if the piping system is not properly maintained and the people are not increasing their labor productivity as a result of health improvement from use of protected water, then the gains from the water project is unclear.

In addition to exploring what can be done with aid to counter the Dutch disease for resource rich members of the cesspool, Collier notes how badly the oil and mineral rich African countries have done, perhaps never to come out of the cesspool.

This monograph attempts to present the specific case of the *aid-dependent economy* and explore the possibility for its extrication from the cesspool. The central idea is *good-governance government*, which must be a necessary condition for any development aid to an aid-dependent economy. The main finding of the study can be stated as a *derivative* of the transaction cost theorem (not to confuse with the Coase theorem):

> *Irrespective of the source and the manner of aid management, aid for a non-good-governance government above the food-aid threshold tends to increase transaction costs to infinity. Such aid is "destructive" aid, and donor's withdrawal of it becomes transaction cost reducing for the aid-recipient.*

The aid received cannot fall below the food-aid threshold since that implies the population dies; that level of aid is now received unconditionally and is a part of the UN human rights declaration.

Arab aid to Ethiopia has gone to fund sectarianism and against the non-Moslem population. The above result is particularly relevant for emerging economies such as China and Russia, who may want to do what the Soviets did by way of aiding *independent African countries* and failed. China and Russia can help Africans in the dangerous cesspool by withdrawing their aid; or better still by coordinating their aid with G^4 and its food-aid threshold conditionality.[1]

Only aid coming from a good-governance government source, which is subject to the food-aid conditionality is acceptable to the Ethiopians, and generally to the food-aid dependent population of the Horn of Africa area. There are at least four major reasons why the global good-governance government may succeed to win the Ethiopian or the Horn of Africa case. First, Since 13 of the 17 years rule by the Derg were devoted to the destruction of private economy and society, the Ethiopians have an opportunity to start from a scratch – just like Germany and Japan did after the end of the Second World War – by first establishing good-governance government. There is no inherited wealth or property over which to quarrel, only destruction all over the place.

Second, G^4 has complete control over the main political actors of the place. It negotiated with the Soviets to leave the area, with the Derg to

---

[1] The food-aid conditionality can also be called the development-aid conditionality since it has the same ruling for any development aid (i.e. aid above the food-aid threshold).

disband (both outside its, i.e. G^4's, immediate control) and installed the governments in Asmara and Addis Ababa, who depend entirely on aid they receive from G^4. All the relevant and official opposition parties in the country depend on aid and support coming from G^4. All the elite of society are protected by G^4 both inside Ethiopia and outside in the Diaspora. Increasing numbers of Ethiopians (as many as a quarter of the total population today), which is also equally true of the population of the Africa Horn area generally, are food-aid dependent.

In the meanwhile and thirdly, G^4 appears to tighten its control of the Horn of Africa area including Ethiopia. It has created conditions that make it impossible for an "independent" government to emerge in the area. In addition to dividing the people two-ways, the rulers both in Addis Ababa and Asmara are left with ungovernable situations. To this must be added the stranglehold through the NATO forces presence in Djibouti, which, while making it impossible for an independent government to emerge in Addis Ababa, it also puts a burden on G^4, i.e. a moral burden to protect the legitimate interests of Ethiopia regarding access to the sea and against adversarial excesses of the Arab world, including the shipment of arms, personnel and money to funnel sectarianism and lawlessness in the area. It is the Arab States that were in the forefront of Ethiopia's dismemberment with their overt support for Eritrean independence.[2]

Where does this control of the situation by G^4 lead to? The monograph probes this question and points to a general direction of solutions. Fourth and finally, of all the major problems G^4 is confronted with in the World today, the case of the aid-dependent economy is the easiest and least costly to solve. For G^4 it is a challenge to combat and to overcome as well as an opportunity worth taking.

---

[2] It is interesting to note that some Arab governments including the Arabic Sudanese Government were actively supporting the breakup of the Ethiopian state and denying its legitimate access to the sea, although there is no evidence of Ethiopian aggression toward the Arabs.

1. Some Sources of Transaction Cost Growth: The Derg Regime

The overthrow of the Ethiopian Monarchy in 1974 made a stop to three decades of market reform and sustainable development, which started toward the end of the Second World War. A new period of "economic reform" *without Economics and Economists* ensued in 1974 under the direction of the Derg, as the military communist government is commonly known in Ethiopia. The Derg undertook extensive policy measures, which made markets inefficient or destroyed them. The process which continued to this day resulted in the non-existence of certain markets and desfunctionality of all markets as well as continued underdevelopment of the economy. Whether government acts out of "ignorance" or on the basis of deliberative intent, the primary focus of the following discussion is on the analysis of observed market operations and transaction costs in a society beset by traumatic change.

1.1 Even Under Feudalism Transaction Cost Rationale can be a Basis of Economic Decision Making

Looked at from a Coasian perspective, the problems presented in Box 1 can be analyzed using transaction cost economics. Beletu's restaurant is not exactly in the mould of a firm or business organization of the Coasean world. Beletu's restaurant lacks hierarchy or the internal structure to match the M- and H- modes of modern business organizations of a market economy. It also does not match a sole proprietorship in a market economy because the paraphernalia of business law, public policy and bureaucracy to enforce the law and contracts, which are important determinants of business organizations and market outcomes, are missing in part or in whole in Beletu's case.

Box 1: Biting the Hand That Feeds One

During the 1960s (the period before the Derg) you could walk to Beletu's restaurant (fictitious) and upon payment of 0.50 Birr (equal to USD 0.20) have a hefty meal. Beletu obtained the *teff* (millet) from her farm; she used her own labor and the free labor of relatives and servants. The house or restaurant was hers as well. Beletu offered a range of foods to the client under strict observance of church rules and practices. In pricing the food she sold, Beletu did not add these major material input and labor costs in food production. Although she perhaps might not know it, Beletu was more a philanthropist, a sharing individual, than a businessperson.[3] Whereas this was the true story, of who Beletu was and of what she did, the Derg executed her for being a "feudalist exploiter". None of those thousands, perhaps tens of thousands, of customers who benefited from her "subsidized" foods ever came forward to speak on her behalf at her "trial" or killing rituals. It is not Beletu alone that was killed; there were many others like her who perished in the same way.[4] The restaurant industry was destroyed, and human rights grossly violated and truth and justice sacrificed by organized and armed criminals who captured the state machinery by force of arms. The criminal nature of that government did not change because the Derg became the Workers Party of Ethiopia, or the dictator became the Chairman of the communist party.

Beletu herself does not match the description of Coasean "entrepreneurial coordinator". She succeeded to organize production on the basis of both market and non-market rules. She may have made some heuristic calculations in order to determine price, and acceptable or tolerable "loss" levels from her restaurant business, given that she could not earn positive profits from the operation. She was also responsive to market signals, for example, buying more of market goods such as salt, pepper, spices, fish, chicken, butter, etc. when the prices drop and buying fewer quantities of the market goods when their prices rise. The market itself was incapable of sending correct market signals and needed sustainable reform including legislation, institutions, civic education, etc., in order to do that. If Beletu were a Coasean entrepreneurial coordinator, she would be expected to charge a marginal cost price under competition or a monopoly price (a marginal revenue equal to marginal cost price) where it is applicable.

What happens when people are so poor, they cannot pay marginal cost prices for food, let alone paying the higher marginal revenue equal to marginal cost price under monopoly? Beletu is faced with no demand for her food at a price equal to marginal cost and she found a purpose in life

---

[3] Did Beletu know that the cost of production of food (equal to value added) in her restaurant should be less than the price charged for food in the market? That, you may recall, is the Coaesean justification for the firm (or Beletu's restaurant in this case).

[4] It is estimated that Ethiopia lost in this way over a million of its elites under the Derg.

by sharing her God's gift with her fellowman and is drawn into thinking and acting that way by the teachings of the Ethiopian Orthodox Church. The true reason why the Derg killed her and people like her will perhaps never be known. It also proved hopeless and purposeless for the regime to attempt to use the professions and professionals to prove that Beletu was an "exploiter" because she wasn't. Whether the death penalty should or should not be applicable in any case at all, or whether it should not be applicable to Beletu's case in particular is another matter. The law, politics, religion, philosophy and sociology have perhaps more to offer than economics in those matters.

1.2 Abolishing Markets as a Method of Reducing Transaction Cost

Box 2 and 3 illustrate that government can knowingly or unknowingly create conditions for transaction costs to increase. Either way, government is not playing a constructive role: is not using public policy and public property to enhance private property development.

Box 2: Tufa's Eggs Business

Ato Tufa (fictitious) was one among many individuals who made a living by collecting eggs from the villages around Addis Ababa and selling them to consumers in the large city. Tufa collected the eggs in some containers, hand-carried them for a distance of over ten kilometers to reach the town. He had a few established customers but otherwise walked through the city alleys the whole day until he sold his consignment. Own labor cost did not figure in his cost calculations and the margin that kept him going must have been a small one. Tufa could not afford to wear manufactured shoes, a sign of low earning capacity from his trade.

At a time when each member of the ruling military junta considered himself as a head of state, and any announcement they made on the media was the equivalent of a government decree, decision was made to fix the price of eggs and to control the movement of people. The effect of this government move against Tufa and many like him was immediate. Small traders in eggs, Tufa amongst them, stopped their operation and eggs became expensive and often unavailable to consumers in the town.

There are always the needs for reform in both developed market economies and developing non-market economies. One would assume there is perhaps a relatively greater cost to reform market operations in a developing non-market economy than in a developed market economy. This is because the reforms required in a developed market economy are incremental; whereas the market reforms in a developing economy (including China and Russia) are in the nature of total change or transformation, in the sense that reforms have to be made in many areas concurrently – including the system of governance, the organizational structure of firms, market structures, government legislation and the protection of human and property rights, and most importantly, perceptions and social values. Some of these changes are long run changes and involve relatively large cost outlay.

One of the things that society can do is search for ways of minimizing transaction costs by planning and making optimum use of the opportunities created for such purposes now. For a developing country like Ethiopia there are today the Structural Adjustment or successor Programs, the Millennium Development Goal strategy, the WTO and UNDP support schemes and other bilateral and multilateral, financial, material and technical assistance programs to benefit from. Any market reform is expected to reduce transaction costs, and destruction of markets for *economic goods* cannot be transaction cost reducing.[5]

Box 3: Market Destruction as a Method of Eliminating Transaction Costs

> A revolutionary leader in a regional city summoned members of the newly commissioned local price control committee, composed of representatives of the Ministry of Commerce and Industry, city elders, and revolutionary cadres to assemble at the regional city's cattle market, where he had built kraals. Each kraal is marked by a price-poster. The leader had earlier deployed armed guards to force the cattle traders, as they drove into the city, to bring their cattle to the kraals in the city market. As soon as the traders arrived at the kraals, they surrendered their animals to the revolutionary pricing committee; which immediately proceeded to register the animals and the respective owner, determined the price of each animal, and then placed them in the designated kraals. Customers were supposed not to

---

[5] This may be differentiated from markets for economic bads (such as markets for drugs, crime, etc.), which may be destroyed to reduce transaction costs and for the good of society.

waste time bargaining. The sales price of each animal was clearly labeled, and all that the customer needed to do was make his/her choice, pay the price and take away the animal. The cattle trader was supposed to collect his money at the end of the day less government service charge. Neither the cattle traders nor the customers had asked for the "government service"; and the next market day no trader drove his cattle to the city kraals and no customer turned up.

Soon after that, information reached everybody that a "traditional" cattle market has opened up just outside the city and people were flocking to the new market, when the revolutionary guards disbanded it and confiscated the animals, as punishment for not respecting "government order". That ended the cattle market in the city and banished the cattle trader. People had to endure the inconvenience of discovering through word of mouth an animal for sale and buy it at the place of the owner or seller, perhaps under the cover of darkness, to avoid being caught by a government agent.

Market destruction represents the maximum social loss of benefits engendered by such adverse policy selection. One can try to drive people back to Stone Age in order to minimize transaction costs for society, but the destruction of markets is no solution to the problem for a society capable of calculating transaction cost in terms of loss or social benefits and opportunities forgone by the destruction of markets

1.3 Induced Market Inefficiency as a Source of Transaction Costs

Transaction costs and market failures can sometimes result from government decisions (see Box 4). In market models where the government variable is exogenous (or endogenous at the level of good-governance government) information asymmetry, market structure, and agents' opportunistic behavior are considered important sources of transaction costs; and reform or government policy intervention is sought in order to eliminate or reduce transaction cost. However, *market inefficiency* can also be introduced by government action and policy.

In this example, individuals incur transaction costs in the form of search costs (to find out what the new directives for public stores are, which change by the day, or who are entitled to buy what from those stores, what and where the next consignment of merchandise would be delivered, searching for the black markets available to trade the goods and services that customers want, etc.); and bargaining costs as when the buyer negotiates with the seller for the best buy in the stock, for the right neck measurement in the shirt, or for better complements offered by the shop. Black markets introduce a new array of transaction costs – search and information costs are high and risks of being caught and punished while operating in illegal markets are also high. Black market prices reflect these uncertainties and risks. Black markets are also viewed as relatively efficient markets since they are used as outlets for products without alternative markets.

Box 4: Forced to Buy More Than What One Bargained For – An Aspect of Market Disfunctionality

Addis Ababans under the Derg regime bought certain things only from the few government stores that dotted the town, which held limited stocks of merchandise. You might go there, let us say, to buy a mattress. At the counter you were told by any one of a large number of attendants that you could buy the mattress provided you also bought a T.V. antenna; and, if you turned up on another day, a couple of kettle lids. You may have no choice in the matter if you needed the mattress. For some it was better if the store management added the prices of the antenna or kettle lids to the price of the mattress and charged them the total, and by so doing saved them the trouble of carrying home things they did not need.

The practice was widespread. The fruit vendor would have nice bananas for sale hanging, but when you went to buy it, you were told to buy a kilo of rotten orange for every kilo of the banana you wanted to buy. Making a scene of it did not help and could result in a "revolutionary measure"[6] being taken against you. If the trader chose to be helpful, he might tell you that was how he got it from the government distributors. You went to the Kebele shop to buy salt and you could be instructed to buy some pencils along with the salt; edible oil and then required to buy also something or other that the shop kept and was not selling.

---

[6] "Revolutionary measure" could mean death by shooting, arrest and detention, or any other punitive action arbitrarily taken against individuals by a government agent.

1.4 Nationalization, Public Enterprises and Escalating Transaction Costs

Transaction cost economics can shed some light on the workings of *public enterprises* in non-market economies. Public enterprises in the Ethiopian case (see Box 5) did not arise from government policy to provide alternative sources of supply for goods and services, as for example, the state establishing a nuclear plant to supply electricity, a rail or air service in an industrialized market economy, because private markets do not exist for those services. In the Ethiopian case, public enterprises under the Derg emanated from the government sweeping nationalization program of private property including commercial farms, wholesale trade, manufacturing firms, land, extra houses[7], and schools. Private properties existed in the pre-Derg period, when these "firms" operated as de facto sole proprietorships or limited liability companies on the bases of the business laws of Ethiopia. Under the Derg regime government enterprises automatically lost their identity and economic rationale.

One may point to the Soviet Union or Cuba for inspiration, but what these countries had were unique experiences which were not communicable in the form of theories, innovations and technological transfers through trade and industrial relocation. Design of business organizations or firms for sustainable production was not the objectives of the Hun Empire builders – it was military conquest. The soviet system for production was based on planning for group effort like in war economics, where the individual is not the object of the plan, but winning the war or the economic challenges of capitalism was.

Coase saw the firm as a system of long-term contracts. One does not establish a production facility without the commitment to put in whatever it takes in order to ensure there is an acceptable rate of return from the investment over the long term. The Coasean entrepreneur operates in an environment which is fully under his/her control. In making his/her decisions the entrepreneur takes into account the "outside environment", like the business law, political stability, competition, social values, etc. In

---

[7] Individual ownership was restricted to a single house, and all extra houses were nationalized. By a circular, government set a ceiling to the house floor - not more than $180\ m^2$.

the case of the Soviet enterprises, on the other hand, neither the management nor the workers in the enterprise determine the fate of the enterprise; they are there to implement the plan produced for them by the Central Committee of the Soviet Union. If they had some lee way in their daily activities in the enterprise, it derives from whimsical dictates of the "boss", nothing firm, stable, formal or transparent about it, and there is nobody taking responsibility for it, especially if it turned out to be problematic.

With such public enterprises owned by the Derg regime, the financing of these economic organizations and activities were not rationally explained. How did the government acquire the resources to pay for normal recurrent and capital expenditures of government, and for all these economic enterprises and activities, which were brought into the spheres of government ownership and control? These were resources taken away from the people illegally. That was done by condemning property owners and private properties, and making the owners of property and their system of economic management the causes of the underdevelopment of the economy. Over a million of Ethiopia's elite were killed by the Derg and the economy, which was having a sustainable growth rate before the Derg, plummeted to irrecoverable low levels and rates of growth under the Derg.

The Regime's enterprises or "firms" lacked mission, stable management and even personnel,[8] and their financing did not come from own, i.e. firm- or enterprise-operation, but from the Treasury. Toward the end of the Derg era, the orientation of the public enterprises was to supply food (canned foods), uniforms, and bullets [9] for the campaigns which can only be described in retrospect as campaigns against the people.[10] As many

---

[8] Many activities in the collectivist system are carried out as "campaigns". Thus, to hold the celebration of the coming to power of the revolutionary government, arches are erected on roads in and out of Addis Ababa using imported material and work force commandeered from government departments, kebeles in the city and peasant associations. After the day of celebration those arches are left where they are and nobody owns them or has responsibility of any kind over them.

[9] The infrastructure for a defense industry was under construction at the time while the "bullets" were supplied from the Soviet Union.

[10] Since all these are carried out in secret by unknown forces for some unexplained objectives (i.e. unknown to the Ethiopian people), economists and all professionals are left with nothing to explain. Among the rumours widely circulated at the time was the

independent, donor assisted and government approved study reports showed, most of the state farms and other government enterprises remained bankrupt for all the period under the Derg.

In theory the *private* enterprise owner/manager had a (legal) occupational status, title-deeds to land or uncontested claims to property and accountability and responsibility for any decision or action taken. As shown in Box 1, under a market system the enterprise manager kept the wage bill as low as possible by limiting to a minimum the extent of wage-employment and using unpaid family and own-labor as well as other own resources like the *Teff*, the house and covering utility costs in Beletu's case – all transaction cost reducing measures.[11] Since the practice of absorbing such costs by private operators under conditions of stiff competition among suppliers (who became irrational and failed to declare bankruptcy and close their businesses, such as Beletu) was widely practiced, the true price of food in Beletu's case was not reflected by market prices. Nevertheless, market price was the measuring rod for market performance, which all market participants whether buyers or sellers, including Beletu's rational-half, watched and obeyed.

What Box 5 shows is that Derg's public enterprise managers were *expected* to be responsive not to market signals, the law, contracts and sense of professionalism but to the whimsical dictates of the ruler who has placed himself in the status of a demigod.

Very few of them claim they held positions in government which they can say allowed them to make positive contributions to the development of the Ethiopian economy. They may say they endured under difficult circumstances and that they have done the best they could for themselves and society. Most, however, perished because they clashed with the dictator or his cronies over principles. Others left the country in search of work and a place where they can live in peace and with dignity

---

existence of a "plan" (whose plan? No answer) to develop Ethiopia so that it will be in the front row, with Cuba, the USSR, China, N. Korea and Albania as well as others under the fold of the group in the fight against imperialism. In the meanwhile, the Derg was busy cleaning the house, inventing and destroying the enemy from within – such as the feudalists, bureaucrats, imperialist agents, exploiters, etc.

[11] Please note that in many industrialized economies it is illegal to use labour without a legal contract.

The cost to society engendered by misuse and abuse of professions and professionals should also be noted. The government and/or the power manager in the example of Box 5 may be unaware of the wider implications of what they were doing. By posturing as a farm manager, the electrical engineer, let us say the power manager was professionally, has in a sense put to shame the agriculture minister in the eyes of the dictator and the indoctrinated public. He may not also realize that by his action he has helped in the destruction of the bureaucracy, and the rule of law, which had taken so much time, commitment, manpower and generosity of donors to create and build. The power manager, by that one act, has succeeded to replace the ministers and ministries of civil service, labor and social affairs, state farms, agriculture and commerce and trade as well as do away with the law, bureaucratic procedures and his own contractual duties and responsibilities.

The rule of law is substituted by the rule of the jungle. The dictator approves of the power manager's effort because he saw a magnification of his personality or his own replica in the manager, which he perhaps felt is not a threat to him personally.

The manager may have also acted opportunistically in response to the strong signals that come from the dictator, which reads: "follow me, I am the law, the government, the high court judge, the moral teacher, the beneficent, the demigod!."

Box 5: Nationalization of Bakeries, Schools and Farms

In a period of one to two years Around 1975 the Derg regime nationalized private properties, including private manufacturing firms, wholesale trade, extra houses,[12] farms and schools (Mulat, 1993). The adverse effect of this government policy on output growth was immediate. Famine, which was a local phenomenon and mitigated by peasant coping strategies before 1975, became generalized after 1975, covering most of the country's geographical space and population, and requiring the intervention of the international community with massive food aid.

---

[12] By legislation the Derg confiscated urban property. The individual can own only one house, and by a circular there was a ceiling to the area of the house.

> The economic effect of nationalization of bakeries, farms and schools had been similar, and included public sector employment growth, soaring wage bill, rising costs of production, monetization of government deficits, and economic bankruptcy. For example, an immediate effect of nationalization of the private bakeries[13] in Addis Ababa was to increase the personnel size and increase exponentially the cost of operation of the enterprises.
>
> The case of the Power Authority[14] illustrates a common problem in public enterprise management in non-market economies. The manager of the Power Authority witnessed idle land around the dams generating electricity which were under his control and the manager decided to operate irrigation farms and market the produce. From the proceeds of these farms, the manager of the power authority was able to purchase agricultural inputs, recruit wage laborers, build stores and even supply transport. He also found the creative use of his talent was recognized not only by the workers in the authority who were the direct beneficiaries from the weekly delivery of farm outputs but also by the ruler of the country who was quick to make the whole nation know the exemplary conduct of the power authority manager. Imagine the farm workers asking for a raise of their pay, or the new enthusiastic farm manager, appointed by the power manager, using his influence to expand agricultural production for exports. What is the role of the agriculture minister? How legitimate is the posturing of the power manager as farm manager? How do you determine farm output prices and the pay for farm workers? What happens to the farm and all that is in it and associated with it if the power manager died in a car accident? The economist cannot prevent the power manager from trying but the folly of the whole episode is there for everyone to see as an afterthought or a lesson from the past.

The bureaucracy, the courts, the parliament, the police, and the people are incapacitated by the gang rule which eventually evolved to a one-man

---

[13] Although some bakeries were kept in the hands of the previous owners, they operated as government enterprises, with no room for independent decision-making. Costs of production soared by the conversion of all workers in the bakeries into wage employees, by expanding employment unrelated to the enterprise's ability to pay or work needs and by use of new technologically ill-adapted machinery and equipment which left extensive excess capacities. In agriculture, seasonal workers under private farm management became government permanent employees with all benefits in addition to regular pay, under government control.

[14] Fictitious, for illustration purposes

rule, because they are incapable of sending corrective signals (such as arresting the power manager and penalizing him for his misdeeds) that can guide the dictator, power manager and society. The government has also successfully destroyed opposition to the dictator's rule and closed down or banished civil society organizations and the free media. Physical elimination using the cover of constitutionalism, the law, protection of the interests of the state, and some fake court proceedings constituted the common method used by the Derg for containing such threats to power.

However, *intent* is difficult to define or get at the individual level. At the collective level it may at least be possible to show the variation between expressed goals (as a measure of intent) and actual achievement. Individual intentions are not primary objects of inquiry in information asymmetry. For economic analysis it is the observed results of human action that matter the most. Thus, if the power manager were asked whether or not he responded to the "signals" of the dictator and dominance of opportunism, he most probably would contest that. For example, he would argue that at a time when millions of Ethiopians were starving, including his own co-workers in the authority, he felt the compulsion to do something about the human suffering, irrespective of what bureaucratic responsibility entails. The alternative would be to do nothing like most other government officials at the time. Contracts in that system are not prime movers, and as a matter of fact, contracts are irrelevant to the system. The system in which the power manager worked and lived is governed by unwritten rules. His conscience, the power manager claims, is clear and he would do what he did given another opportunity. But if society would like to punish him for not respecting his employment contract which did not exist, so be it. His only crime as far as he is concerned is producing some food from a piece of land that otherwise would have remained idle, and give employment to people who would have remained unemployed had it not been for his action. These are strong points and nobody can prove the power manager's intention has been to the contrary.

Part of the failings of that system had thus been the absence of a good-governance government and indeed the absence of rule of law, a situation created by the Derg regime. There is wide scope for opportunism in the system, however, but not the kind of opportunistic behavior one observed in the Coasean world. In the Coasean world there are opportunistic behaviors that are legal and beneficial to society. Public policy is directed to nurture these and to strengthen their application by legislation or provision of government services, such as training, information dissemination, licensing, etc. Thus, cooperation by the public to protect the environment or to fight drugs and criminal behavior are in the nature of positive opportunism. The individual indulges in such actions and activities out of self-interest, but by so doing advances also the interest of the larger society.

Negative or destructive opportunism is represented by individual or group criminal actions which are prosecutable by law. Government intervention to contain those types of opportunistic behaviors includes legislation and law enforcement. But all opportunistic behaviors are not prosecutable. If you witnessed a harmless woman being robbed by a gang of thieves, nobody is going to accuse you for watching the crime, except perhaps your conscience. Even in this case there is a role for government in the Coasean world. Government can and should pave the way, through legislation, civic education and other forms of encouragement in support of moral society (e.g. the civil society in defense of human rights, the religious societies, the free media, law enforcement agencies, etc.) so that it can be able to operate legally in peace and freedom.

2. Privatization and Transaction Costs

Many African countries participated in the implementation of the so-called Structural Adjustment Program (SAP), an evolving program, coordinated by the World Bank and the International Monetary Fund.[15] Post-Derg Ethiopia was one of them. The program initially consisted of market reform, a phrase to mean all economic activities should be managed by market rules; public sector reform, to give purpose for public policy and public property development as means of enhancing private property development; and political reform, to establish good-governance governments. SAP also included a package of economic reforms including privatization program, price, tax, sectoral, trade and investment reforms.

It is difficult to measure economic success for any African country, whether or not the country is implementing SAP. However, for SAP countries, statistical measurements give mixed results, there is economic growth when resources in the form of aid, credits, FDIs flow in, and relapses when the inflow is reduced or ceases. *The problem is basically with the dysfunction of government, markets and firms and in their relationships*, and transaction cost economics (or neo-institutional economics) can provide some answers to this puzzle.

The neo-institutional economics prescription for the role of government is this: government undertakes public policy and public property development with the objective of enhancing and complementing the development of private property. Among its wide ranging policy arsenal government uses signaling (*honest signals*)[16] to correct market failure, to

---

[15] There are many bilateral and multilateral assistance programmers for Ethiopia outside the SAP which are based on the SAP arrangement

[16] *Honest signals* indicate *true goals*. *Deceptive signals* never help achieve or yield *true goals*. A politician with a religious, tribal or racist agenda accuses the political opposition party or parties for representing minority interests. The aim is to appeal to the majority electorate (say 99 percent of the total electorate) who has already developed, in the views of the politician, resentment and hatred against the minority one percent. This is a case where *an honest signal* (the accusation against the minority one percent) *is* used to obtain the true goal, which is extracting retribution from the minority one percent. But if the electorate (especially the one percent) believes that the society is integrated and there is no class division on the basis of religion, race or tribe, then the politician looses the elections, even though the politician has sent honest

attain economic efficiency, and social justice; and in general to create conditions favorable for a sustainable development of private property. But, as the following examples show improper use of signaling prevents the attainment of goals and increases the cost of programs and activities for society.

---

signals. This represents political behaviour in a developed democracy, where the society, cognizant of its democratic values, knows the implication of having such a politician as a leader is the destruction of economy and society.

One may then ask "what if the politician were actually trying to do good but believes his society has perverse values, and in order to solve the ills of that society he produced signals (deceptive signals) that make him attractive or acceptable by the society?" In that case, the politician is using *deceptive signals*, which will never yield or bring about the true goal of society as he now sees it, because the true goal of that society which elected him to office is the destruction of the minority one percent.

The test for a mature democracy arises when the politician appears democratic, egalitarian, and just, thus representing the values of the democratic society (use deceptive signals) to be elected and once in power to implement his hidden agenda, which is the destruction of the minority one percent. The strategy of the politician is to replace the true goal of society (the goal for which the society will vote for him) with his true goal which is totally destructive by deceptive signaling. The intention of the politician is not known to society, and society needs to have the opposition, free media, and all types of legitimate civil society organizations as well as be vigilant to expose the politician and reject him early in the game. By so doing society saves itself and proves that the true goal of the society (which is not the true goal of the politician) can only be realized by "honest signals", it can never be reached or achieved by "deceptive signals".

These two cases above, where the politician uses deceptive signaling, represent the political education programme in which Ethiopian politicians are sucked in today. It is like asking what to do if your father robbed or killed to feed his family. Those Ethiopians brought up in Christian and Islamic traditions condemn the robber or the murderer, irrespective of his or her station in society or the place in the family. The politician who chose to talk in "codes" or use deceptive signals in order to save society and the society that accepted the murderer and the liar must pay the price for its mistakes. That is precisely why society demands the free press, the civil society organizations, NGOs and good-governance government. If politicians don't have an extremist or a tribal agenda they should not accept a tribal label and embrace a tribal liberation program and waste the rest of their life explaining their position. Read about the history of the All Ethiopia Unity Organization, and other non-ethnic parties and their relationship with the ruling EPRDF.

2.1 Government and Bureaucracy

The current Ethiopian Constitution[17] is divided into two parts: one part deals with a transcription of the United Nations Bill of Human Rights, and the other part is an adaptation from the Stalinist and Apartheid/colonialist formulation of the rights of "peoples, nations and nationalities." A careful study of this crafty work reveals that the intention is to create confusion by whoever wants to use the constitution. Let us say the intention of the user or signaler is to advance democratic practice at a regional or state level government. That requires regional level participation, and when a state level group organizes for that purpose, it finds itself blocked by the federal level rulers using the UN bill of human Rights and private property rights and its protection as the justification for their actions. Similarly, when an individual or a group seek to advance the cause of human rights and private property development they find themselves blocked by the "state government" and the federal government would use the rights of "peoples, nations and nationalities" and non-interference in regional affairs as a justification for its stand in the matter (see Box 6).

Using simple analytical filters, one discovers asymmetric information as the source for the confusing signals. Whoever is using the signals (the rights of peoples, nations and nationalities; non-interference in regional or state affairs; human rights and private property rights and protection; etc.) is deliberately blocking critical information from reaching the public, which is that the regional government is owned by the federal government and all officers in charge in the regional or state governments are employees of the federal government, paid and directed by the federal government. In both cases (i.e. the UN Bill of Human Rights and the rights of peoples, nations and nationalities) signaling is used to create a zero sum game: there will be no progress in the advancement of the

---

[17] Some constitutions in the developing world are fashioned on religious books and with some additions from esoteric cosmology and help from dedicated disciples, these constitutions can easily grow into a theology – i.e. become an all-time true divine revelations. Constitutions, however, are manmade and to be revised and amended. This unfortunate development (the tendency to regard constitutions as divine revelations) does not reflect the character of the Ethiopian people, who have differentiated constitutions from the holy books (for them the Bible and the Holy Koran) over 500 years ago; see translations from *Geez* by the prominent scholar Getachew Haile of the work of Aba Bahri and some episodes from *Dekike Estifanos* (martyrdom of the religious followers of Aba Estifanos).

peoples, nations and nationalities and retrogression occurs with respect to human rights and development of private property.

Individuals are appointed to high government post on the basis of ethnic origin or religion. The idea behind is demonstration of a democratic practice in government – democracy as a broad representation in government of diverse ethnic and religious groups in the country. The effect of this on employment contract and on bureaucratic performance is given low priority in the eyes of the appointer. The individual sends messages, informing on ethnic or religious background, possibly together with some education or work experience to signal eligibility, and the recipient of the signals (government or political party) provides employment to the signaler.

As another example, a professor is assigned to a professional post such as chief research officer of an HIV-AIDS research institute, but the professor could be a Ph.D. in theology and a novice for the job. The aim of the appointment may be to signal professionalism at the workplace. There are two ways of viewing the signaling problem in this case. One way is to view government as the "ignorant party" who makes an adverse selection (a pre-contract problem) by employing the professor by mistake, for example, government was duped by the kinds of deceptive signals transmitted by the professor. The cost to society is the loss of professional service for the duration of the employment of the professor, plus the cost of introduction of greater vigilance and improvement of the job screening mechanism to handle future employment.[18] This is tolerated under any situation, and a good-governance government uses the occasion to reform, for example, introducing a relatively more efficient job screening. It all means that government is made more efficient as a result.

The second way deals with the question "what happens when government operates with prior information about the signal and deliberately screens the professor for the job?" It does this by emphasizing the title "professor" and hiding from public knowledge that the person is a professor of theology, or appointing him professor in order to use deceptive signaling. In this case the cost to society is beyond moral

---

[18] It is assumed that other costs such as negative fallouts, e.g. confusion and sectarianism introduced by the professor during his employment at the place of work are zero.

hazard,[19] and quite literally can grow to infinity. Government is avoiding reliable signals deliberately.[20] The reason why transaction cost tends to infinity is because the objective or the truth will never be arrived at, or the controversy will never get closure, so long as deceptive signals are used (see theorem). Deceptive signals require filters and decoders in order to interpret the true message of the signaler, which could be very costly. When the signal recipient, in this case government, is a party to a hideous design of this sort,[21] no corrective measures are taken, because the government has literally paralyzed parliament, controlled the political opposition, and the bureaucracy for a perpetual mismanagement and siphoning off of public funds.

Dictatorships, ethnocracies, and theocracies operate on this basis and no sustainable private property development is expected in those systems. If the resources are squandered from domestic budget, they continue the downward spiral until total collapse. If the resources to squander are sought in the form of foreign aid, credits and technical assistance, it does not make any sense for the donor community to finance corruption and wastefulness in a poor country.

Foreign direct investments (FDIs) can only go where the investors are guaranteed a *satisfycing* and sustainable return on their investment. Only a good-governance government can guarantee that. However, theocracies and dictatorships can at best attract neo-colonialist and mafia types of "businesses". But these are systems of economic pillage which impoverish the population of the recipient countries. The rulers might gain; but then judging by African modern history nearly all of its dictators never lived to enjoy the loot.

When a former rebel guerilla fighter is appointed to the post of chief of police without accreditation and experience replacing a former graduate of a police academy with years of work experience in the police department

---

[19] As when the "engineer" (in reality not qualified as one) squanders public funds because he is under the protection of the ruler, while not producing the bridge.

[20] The role assigned to government in transaction cost economics is to reduce transaction costs or eliminate them if possible (and not to increase such costs by direct or indirect government action)

[21] This is contrary to the role of government in both neoclassical economics and new institutional economics. The role of government is to generate honest signals.

18

at home and internationally, the message signaled could be to slight the bureaucracy (i.e. the police department or the HIV-AIDS research institute) and to convey the message to all those supportive of the healthy development and professionalization of the bureaucracy that professionalism does not matter, but that loyalty to the promoter or appointer does. No gain can be made by a government which chooses to use deceptive signaling. The replaced officers, and those employees of the bureaucracy who were dismissed in a similar fashion from their jobs have their human rights violated and society is made to suffer from incompetence and lawlessness, which is what the new appointees bring to office.

A disturbing aspect of the above is when government, instead of promoting the development of the independent press, human rights and women rights advocacy groups, trade unions, etc., through legislation, public funding, honest signals (as opposed to deceptive signal which sends false messages), and request for donor technical and financial assistance, chooses instead to establish its own bureaucracy to replace them and to control individual and group behavior. These are not legitimate functions of government, and under a good-governance government the people through their democratically elected representatives must approve the budget, and no people will approve the spending of scarce public resources for a wasteful and destructive cause.

It must be noted that those civil society organizations and advocacy groups take a heavy cost load off the government budget: they make sacrifices to improve social welfare and assist in development without any cost to the government; and it is they and not the government that can evaluate whether or not government assisted them with legislation, licensing, foreign grants, etc. Foreign grant or credits to assist government in the establishment of parallel bureaucracy (replacement for civil society organizations, rights advocacy groups, etc.) is not expected in the new world order.

Ethiopian high government officials (not all of them) and their subordinates following their example attend long-distance education programs or take courses at Addis Ababa University, while in office. At the same time qualified and experienced Ethiopians in the respective areas of training aspirations of the officials are unemployed, dismissed from jobs and forced to leave their country in search of work. Here too analytical filters are needed in order to interpret the "true" messages of the confusing signals.

The individual government officials cannot be blamed for seeking education. In fact their action may well be interpreted as positive opportunism if they used their own finances, won free scholarships and their *contracts* allow them to do it. But if the shield of high office is used for taking public money to pay for their education they have committed a public offence. They also have committed a public offence if they are instrumental or directly involved in denying the people of Ethiopia the services of professionals and closed the bureaucracy to block professional Ethiopians from exercising their rights. If the international community were to point out to the Ethiopian government these failings, it will be construed perhaps as interference in the internal affairs of Ethiopia under the current protocols. But when the Ethiopian government submits a request for international support to expand tertiary education, the donors would have every right to ask "what did you do with educated Ethiopians? Why do you need educated Ethiopians in the future?" and to advise that the Ethiopian government would receive some attention from the donors if it were to request for financial and technical assistance to create productive jobs for educated Ethiopians.

The entire Ethiopian political space is full of "noises" and confusing signals transmitted by government, individuals and groups that require expensive decoders and filters, which the country, living on international food aid, ill affords. The government of Ethiopia is not differentiated from the ruling party, the EPRDF, which controls the legislature, executive and judicial branches of government and acts opportunistically in the manner described above. Some of the political opposition groups are also undergoing an expensive training program on transmitting correct signals and in the art of using deceptive signals. Right now some of them are breaking up[22] because they have a lot more of explaining to do regarding

---

[22] Among these are the many ethnic organizations, which seek to liberate their respective tribes or ethnic groups, without defining the ethnic groups, explaining how and identifying and defining what and from whom they want to liberate themselves. There are others who are paying a heavy price to get their voices heard, who aim to extricate society from the morass of perpetual underdevelopment, degradation, ignorance and poverty. These are not breaking up and are not likely to break up.

their misdeeds than defending the little or nothing good they did to society or the ideals such as democracy, nation-building, human and property right protection, etc.

The role of government is also affected by "outside signals" linking the donors with the Ethiopian government. An important development of the post-2000 era is the officalization and bonding relationship between the Ethiopian government and the donor community. But this bond works non-transparently and lacks a controlled governance structure. As a result, the Ethiopian Government receives signals from the donor community which it tries to decode and respond to. Among the difficulties in this relationship is the role of the officials and functionaries of the donor organizations.

These organizations involve individuals who are utility maximizers within the rules stipulated in their employment contract; and act opportunistically in their dealings with the Ethiopian government. Sometimes although done with the best of intentions the donors or their bureaucratic proxies fail from attaining the goal intended, which is the improvement of the condition of living of the Ethiopian people. The manner of involvement of the donor organizations may also force the Ethiopian government or its officials to act opportunistically, which despite acclaimed intentions may not result in anything good for the Ethiopian people.

One unfortunate development is that the Ethiopian government, which lacks local base or feels it is in full control of the situation in the country and is therefore capable to speak on Ethiopia's interests, reports, not to the Ethiopian people but to the international donors who are trying but have not started to talk with one voice, and on whom the survival of the Ethiopian government depends. The opportunistic behavior of the Ethiopian government exhibits certain messages or data which does not require a wild-goose chase of government intentions in order to analyze.

The Ethiopian government claims the donors' resources are its own and does not produce reports on amounts and sources of specific expenditures for public knowledge. For example, the Ethiopian people are not told how the fuel they consume is financed in a detailed way.[23] If Ethiopians never knew how the Derg's over a million-men war machine was financed,[24] Ethiopian's today have no knowledge of the organization, makeup, size and the financing of the EPRDF military. The production, value and exports of gold is not regularly published in the *Ethiopian Statistical Abstract*, and nothing is reported officially about the parallel government of Ethiopia, made up of powerful people and operating "behind the throne";[25] and if this is not the case now the past arrangement was never explained to the Ethiopian people. There are apartment buildings in town, and there is talk of a dam to construct, roads are built, etc. but the participation of the Ethiopian people, the sources of finance and the property rights associated with these things are not common knowledge.

Under normal circumstances these matters should have been common knowledge, but they were not. One would assume the donors require such reports relating to the use of their aid to be transparently and independently produced (and compared to the Ethiopian government's report if that government chose to report to its people independently) not only for their governing boards and governments, but also for the wider international community. Instead, such reports are prepared by the donors in consultation with the Ethiopian government, trying to give the wrong impression that the Ethiopian government and the Ethiopian people are one and the same.

Again, without going into intentions behind signals, one can analyze variance between signals and intentions from observance of real results of an action. An interesting report[26] from East Timor revealed that donors money of about five billion US dollars (or $ 8000/head) was spent in the past few years and in the meanwhile poverty of the population increased

---

[23] During the Derg period fuel was rationed and although the Derg too never reported to the Ethiopian people, rumours circulate that secret deals have been made between the Soviets and the ruler of Ethiopia to get fuel. One may add that concepts such as the Ethiopian government, the Soviets, and agreements are codes which require decoders and filters to understand in the Soviet or Derg era in Ethiopia.

[24] The Soviet's handled these things in secret.

[25] The collection of unofficial advisors which the US President Andrew Jackson used in parallel with the official cabinet (or "parlor cabinet") is referred to as the *Kitchen Cabinet*.

[26] This was screened by the Aljazeera broadcast station in its "Witness" program of 9 September 2009.

by 14 percent. As to where the money went, the author or authors of the report indicated that over 70 percent of the donors' money was used up by the "international bureaucrats and bureaucracies" and only the remaining portion was used to put up hotels and roads for use by the international bureaucrats among others.[27]

If the Ethiopian government could not report to show such anomaly in the conduct of donor behavior, and seeks working for the coordination of the preparation of such reports, it cannot be to save money, because the donors make available all the money needed in the preparation of those reports. By not telling the truth and not signaling the truth government has increased noise (confusion) or increased deceptive signals and in so doing increased also transaction costs When a simple list of the names and addresses of the beneficiaries From a XHS[28] housing project for urban slum dwellers made public in the private media would be sufficient, drowning the donor and the public in a sea of voluminous reports can only be interpreted as a smokescreen.

Donor money goes to hire a consultant to measure yield elasticity of fertilizer application and for training graduate students in competition policy. If the idea is to provide employment for the consultant and prepare students for future employment, the donor should at least indicate that the purpose of the aid is for those things. The fertilizer is already patented and marketed, and what is needed is "entrepreneurial coordination" to use it in order to create value added and provide productive employment and livelihood to the unemployed masses. Ethiopia is not yet a full member of the WTO and cannot make use or effective use of the duty and quota free import privileges it is given under existing protocols.

In both cases the aid should have gone *quickly*[29] to Argaw who would have transformed economy and society. Argaw's human and property

---

[27] Interestingly, the UN report was showing that living conditions of the Timorese people had improved.

[28] A fictitious donor used here as representing the whole of the donor community in Ethiopia.

[29] "Quickly" is to be stressed because forces are at work in order to change the character of "Argaw" (representing the entrepreneurial forces in Ethiopia) from a hardworking, law-abiding, benevolent and exemplary person into a low-level operative of a criminal mafia gang. That places the whole nation on an irrecoverable course to destruction.

rights were violated by government, be it a state government (Box 6), and in order to live and sustain his family Argaw is forced to work for a mafia group running contraband trade well connected to or in government.

These examples: the XHS housing project, Timorese case, etc. illustrate what we may call a transaction cost theorem (not to be confused with the Coase theorem). The truth in the XHS case can be captured by a list of names and addresses of the beneficiaries of the housing scheme (200? 5000? names and addresses!) and published in the private media (not in authority media). Instead, the authority with whom the XHS concluded the aid agreement uses money provided for by the agreement to prepare "consolidated reports", "expert views and reviews", "technical evaluation reports of the XHS housing scheme" and runs T.V. programs to show what the EPRDF government has done to benefit the people, but never show the evidence on a prior identification and registration list of the people who benefited, and never tell the people that it is XHS money. One can stretch one's imagination and show how infinite amounts of additional Dollar expenditures can go to waste. World class audit firms and engineering firms could be engaged in the production of technical reports on the XHS housing project. Another line of expenditure can go to establish the authenticity of those reports and firms. Now, the donor can choose to pump in money the equivalent of the trillions of Dollars for the recovery program of the world economy meltdown. Even with that it will not be possible to produce the truth about the XHS aid using deceptive signaling. Hence, the *transaction cost theorem*:

> *The truth is beneficial to society, and it can be acquired only by use of honest signals, which cost the least. Transaction cost tends to infinity, if one tries to arrive at the truth using deceptive signals.*

One must remember that the cost of the European Recovery Program or the Marshall Plan, which covered the entire Western Europe, was a mere 13 billion US Dollars.[30] Both the Germans and Japanese must have their most difficult time during the war years and their happiest moment during the recovery period when they rose from the ashes. The best donors could do under the circumstances for Africa is to help Africa see its happiest days, the war period for the continent has been too long. That will be the

---

[30] Marshall Plan – Wikipedia, the free encyclopedia

least costly spending they had to do; if that is not possible, they must at least ensure that their aid is not financing deceptive signals, because that will surely drive Africa into a downward cascading and irrecoverable growth path to disaster.

The effect of these developments on the bureaucracy and private property development is overwhelming. The bureaucracy both at the state and federal level is dysfunctional – everyone in the upper hierarchy may be expert in explaining why, but there is nobody with the courage to accept responsibility. Only a handful of individuals who have broken off from the ruling and other parties have come forward to admit guilt and accept responsibility.

Local level administration is actually bogus, it is there as a part of government arsenal of deceptive signaling (see Box 6). It also is a form of smokescreen directed at the international community who may be inclined to believing that local level administration is practiced in Ethiopia just like in the United States.

But if these "international community" took the trouble of looking in they discover that any state does not have sufficient number of cottage industries to justify a state bureaucracy to service industrial activities. The country does not have a single industry or company that could be described large-scale by West European country standards. The total number of small-scale and cottage industries in the whole country, defined and measured by a European country standards, will be less than a thousand. With that small number, an office given a clear legal mandate, equipped with latest ICT and a handful of professionals would be efficient and cost effective.

Box 6: A Post-Derg Development: Violation of Human Rights and Absence of Property Right Legislation and Protection

Ato Argaw (fictitious) who owned a shop in a small city located some 120 Km outside Addis Ababa was full of hope and, following the overthrow of the Derg regime, immediately went to action to restart a new and hopefully productive life. He expanded his shop and significantly increased his stock of merchandise.

However, Argaw's expectations of efficient public service ("the development of public property and policy meant to enhance private property development") never came, and his hope for individual freedom of action and protection of rights quickly changed into ominous despair. His shop was burgled many times in the past two years by unknown assailants and the police did nothing about it; Argaw suspects undefined members of the police are a party to such crimes. His application to the city administration for a house permit was costly: although he offered gifts and paid bribes directly to the bribe takers and through their intermediaries, his application of four years ago remains unanswered. He was at war with another of the rulers of the newly established government of "peoples, nations and nationalities" who demanded that he supply him from his shop with one thing today and another thing tomorrow without payment. Every time Argaw informed the ruler of the unpaid bills, the ruler simply reminded Argaw to behave with "this is not your region". The truth was that Argaw's forebears arrived first, cleared the forest and settled in a long time ago, long before anybody else arrived there; and in any case, Argaw could not accept the ruler's claim of entitlement to tributes and he could not allow the ruler to violate his human and citizenship rights. To his dismay, though, Argaw discovered a repeat of the violence and thuggery of the Derg, and having nobody to turn to, decided to migrate to Addis Ababa where he felt he might have the protection of the Ethiopian Human Rights Council (EHRC) and the international community.

The shop he left behind was given by the municipality of the "peoples, nations and nationalities" to a cadre from the area that could not run the shop, and because nobody else would rent it for a more productive use, it is allowed to decay. In the meanwhile local kids use it to play hide-and-seek game.

The transaction cost in this narrative includes not only the cost of Argaw's lost property including the house, merchandise and society's loss of use of Argaw's intellectual property, but more importantly the incalculable social loss in the form of degenerative values (destructively opportunistic behavior) of the ethnocracy and its unjust reward system

An Ethiopian small investor (as shown in Box 6) is discouraged by rulers of the ethnocracy (i.e. system of rule of peoples, nations and nationalities). The large investor will waste time and money to get things done (if they can ever be done), while endless exchanges over procedures and responsibilities take place between the state office and federal authorities. The purpose of the federal structure is for deceptive signaling which produces zero sum games. So-called states and regions are the property of the federal government, and their bureaucrats are employees of the federal government. A unitary state such as Japan or France are doing much better and achieving the goals of the states in the US Federation by economizing on resources and personnel.

There is no "federal" bureaucracy that one can point and say "it is working".[31] Recruitmer.t and promotion is made without proper contract, rules and procedures. Fublic service is not readily given to the seeker because decision has to wait the direction of a new appointee, or because the previous official has orderec for computers and people have to wait for the installation and training of staff; and a common obstacle is paused by new departments, high personr.el turnovers, and new assignments which often places the service seeker in a quandary and a fruitless search for information. As a result most departments are intermittently shut down and others so over a prolonged period of time.

The above condition has created a new brand of opportunistic bureaucrats. One type is already described above and consists of poorly trained and inexperienced bureaucrats, who have acquired their position and status in government by signaling ethnic origin, religion, and loyalty to government. Another characteristic the government looks for in prospective job applicants for high positions is capacity to do wrong and take blames on behalf of government. These often try to change things without realizing the full implications of the change. For example, they may try and put to cperation the computerization of the department without realizing that the procedure creates problems, involves wastage

---

[31] Within the framework of SAP and under the cover of public sector reform over 80,000 public servants out of an estimated total of about half a million public sector employees (mostly prcfessionak and top level operatives who secured their employment and positions in the bureaucracy on merit and according to the Central Personnel Agency Regulations cf 1963) were removec from public office by the Transitional and EPRDF Goverrment and replaced by ethnic loyalists and their EPRDF supporters. These destroyed public records, closed offices and opened new ones in the name of reform but apparently carried out for the purpose of pillage of state property and control of political power. Even though the initial leaders of this trend toward de-bureaucratization have left their positions and attempted to cover their tracks by poorly trained replacements, the downward spiral has led to a virtual collapse of the bureaucracy. Tocay most Ethiopians have lost their confidence in the government. A major task of a good-governance government would include putting a stop to this cover-up, corruption and cycle of destruction in government by undertaking reform which must provide closure to past cycles of recriminations and vindictiveness and enhance sustainable economic growth and development. Nobody benefits from the continuation of the destructive course. The reformists are required to come up with a reform agenda and they will be assisted in this task by G^4 and by the relative smallness of state property squandered and fewness of the beneficiaries from destructive opportunism.

and costs as well as new staff or the training of existing staff and requiring synchronization with other departments. They lack the knowledge about the coordinating role of the Civil Service Commission, the law including the establishment legislation of the department they serve and the constitution and had most probably no formal training in public administration or management. Each step they took or decision they made results in complications and transaction costs.

Another type of bureaucrat stays on the job to benefit himself and serve society to the best of his abilities despite the impossible conditions fate has thrown him into, or perhaps he may use the time to review the signals which he transmitted to get the job in the first place, (see Box 5, the case of the power engineer). There is also the elite bureaucrat who knows about these things and does not want to make professional and ethical mistakes, and realizing that his stay in the government post does not get him the right rate of return on his human capital and incapacitates him from giving any useful service to society, works out his next strategic move – use signaling (position in government, educational and work experience) to capture international job, or any other job that gives him peace of mind and a better chance to survive.

Worker moral is an all time low, and workers live in a perpetual fear of being dismissed from work, thus sacrificing their livelihood and endangering their own and their family's lives. They follow their instincts and try to be punctual, and respectful to all those who come seeking public service, although they know very little or nothing gets done. Sometimes they advise people they know not to waste their time by seeking public service. Their opportunistic behavior clearly indicates there is talent and correct ethical behavior which should be tapped by the bureaucracy for the good of everybody. But right now, the department, where they work is not run by rules, and if they are to depend on the good will of the "boss", they loose everything by getting close to the boss when he, as most likely will happen, leaves his post. Which means the workers would like to keep their distance from the boss. Those that want a quick fix may signal their choice for a closer relationship with the boss, but that will be until the boss could write the letter of recommendation they require in an application, give them a raise, a transfer to another unit, or help them with the employment of a relative. This of course invites another strategic move or moves on the part of the boss which complicates further human relationships at the

28

workplace. In an environment devoid of contracts or rule of law transaction costs always tend to cumulate to infinity.

2.2 Denationalization, Firms and Market Behavior

The *privatization* program under SAP coordinated by the World Bank and IMF with the EPRDF government consisted of *denationalization* (return of nationalized property to expropriated Derg victims cr their legal heirs), *institutional reform* (in this case establishment of a privatization agency and passage of a bill), and the *privatization* of public assets or enterprises (transfer of public assets to private operators through sales, service contracts, partnerships, etc.).

Government kept under a new management the relatively larger enterprises such as the Telecommunication Authority, Electricity and Power Authority, etc. for strategic reasons. These were relatively large enterprises providing employment and essential services.

Other enterprises were transferred to regional administrations (not necessarily to all regional administrations). These were consolidated by new additions, mainly in wholesale trade, manufacturing and foreign trade. The so-called regional enterprises and the enterprises kept by the federal government are properties of the federal government because the federal and state governments are the same (a matter that was discussed already). The legal basis for these arrangements, especially the regional public enterprises, is unclear.

There is no clear legal framework for the management of public enterprises in general. The aim is not to apportion responsibility or to determine the legal base for the privatization program. Society needs answers to those legal and organizational questions in order to ensure that scarce resources are efficiently, productively and justly used. The interest of the economist is to show these enterprises and the new additions remain bankrupt,

$$(Re\ venue - Expenditur\ es) < 0$$

and if they are to remain "open", someone must cover cost. If under reform the regional enterprise management were to cut corners and make these enterprises profitable that would be good to society, but this is not possible or sustainable. On the other hand, if the regional enterprises could not be made profitable even under reform and the management decided to close them down to save money that would also be good to society, because the money saved can be used in best alternatives. It will also be good for society if the management were to sell the enterprises to private buyers and if the private buyers, using their "entrepreneurial coordination" abilities were to make them profitable.

All these options are theoretical. In practice the conditions do not exist in order to enable society benefit from the reform measures. The managers are appointed without contract, the public does not even know by whom. Such managers are unlikely to operate with determination; they lack visibility and are lost, seeking direction from the owners that remain unknown even to them. In other words the environment for the exercise of "entrepreneurial coordination" abilities does not exist.

If the public enterprise manager is connected to government, he is likely to figure out there is inherent accountability in the position he holds. His strategy would be to make arrangements to change and move to less accountable but more rewarding positions. Like the bureaucrats reviewed earlier, there are those managers which have little understanding of their positions, and might even be picked by the system, to give directions on reforming the public enterprises. Of course these accelerate the motion toward disaster. They lack the technical knowledge, the experience and also the consciousness demanded by the job (more or less acting like Boxer in the famous satirical novel by Orwell, *Animal Farm*).

It is important that we emphasize the cost to society. The system cannot have competent managers because competent managers are of three types and all of them will not hold the post of public enterprise manager in full view of society. Type 1 is from the system (a member of the ruling party or someone embraced by the party or powerful rulers of the party). It is this fellow who fixes or makes arrangements for a Boxer type to succeed him and he goes for cover. As an insider, he can even pretend to save the situation by assisting the system to get type 2 managers. Type 2 managers can be divided into two groups: type 2A is professional with good track record and attempts to fix things to his best ability but ends up being a scapegoat by the system and its destructively opportunistic behavior. In full view of its media and its "private" press the regime blames the type 2A manager for failing in his duties as manager. There is type 2B, who manipulates corridors of deceit: signaling the authorities with loyalty and professionalism; and signaling the public with honesty, public service and professionalism. For many type 2B operators the job is too demanding, even immoral because they know it is all a waiting game, nothing works however hard they try. They always look for some opportunity to escape from the system.

Type 3 is an accredited professional and independent operator who knows the kind of political environment necessary for him to function. The system too knows that individual will consider it an insult to be asked by the system official to take the job, since most probably he knows of what type 1 did. The system ends no matter which way it turns with Boxer type of managers that can accelerate the journey of the enterprise and all those in it and associated with it to a certain disaster.

The above relates to public enterprises. Property has also gone through the cover of the privatization program to private individuals; and new private companies were introduced following market liberalization under SAP. The government never published a complete list of names and addresses of individuals to whom nationalized property by the Derg has been returned. What it did with villas and apartments left by the Derg is also not made public. The government has not made public the complete list of names and addresses of individuals to whom public property has been transferred by the privatization program. It does not have a complete official registry that is made public of new enterprises formed periodically containing public information such as asset value, ownership structure, line of activity, etc. Since its constitutional pursuit is the protection of the rights of peoples, nations and nationalities, the public naturally expects distribution of private property rights on ethnic classification. That type of information is also unavailable.

An aspect of the use of deceptive signals and destructively opportunistic behavior by government is made apparent by its application of constitutional provisions. Thus, measures can be taken to violate (destructive goal) the private property rights of an individual (case of Ato

Argaw, Box 6) using the clauses in the constitution dealing with the rights of "peoples, nations and nationalities"; and enhancing private property development for *selected individuals and groups*, and justifying non-provision of public registry of enterprises on religion and ethnic origin by the provisions of the constitution dealing with human and property rights.

Private properties operating in this hostile environment are not expected to be productive or profitable. There are no legal, administrative, procedural or commonsense bases for enterprise establishment and for the measurement and determination of enterprise performance. The government tax revenue is collected in the absence of public trail records.[32] In some instances government bureaucracies including the tax offices are closed and new ones opened and the public is made to waste time and effort (incur transaction costs) to get information; which becomes too costly with increased frequency of such changes. The ordinary businessman is left to the mercy of the tax collector, who could use his public position for a destructive end (destructive opportunism). If the taxpayer *is not* from the side of the ruling group then one or more of these obstacles or hurdles can prevent him from attaining his business goal. As an example, we have a case of a tax collector from the office of the peoples nations and nationalities to confront Ato Argaw with onerous tax, which has uncertain legal base, deliberately enacted by the ethnocracy to destroy an entrepreneur who had the potentials for success. Ethiopians have witnessed similar bigotry and denial of human rights and property right protection in schooling, property development (or underdevelopment), land allocation (or misallocation) industrial and business licensing and in public employment.

Even for those individuals and businesspersons on the side of government, these are most difficult times for businesses everywhere. Those among them that have become "entrepreneurial coordinators" in the process realize that keeping their businesses open is harmful to government and society, simply because they save more by closing them down. Those pseudo-businesspersons amongst them require government support (or donor support) to eliminate Argaws (genuine entrepreneurs) from

---

[32] It is common practice for the tax collector to ask the taxpayer to bring tax payment receipts of previous year or years. The tax collector probably got the job, not through competition over qualification, but by signaling tribe, religion, relations with employer, loyalty, etc.

competing against them and would continue acting the role of successful businesspersons using government subsidy, stolen or aid money and running contraband trade under the protection of their government.

Business behavior in Ethiopia today is depicted by Table 1. Because of the unfavorable business climate created by the activities and excesses of those in government and their Pr5 associates, Pr1-Pr4 businesspersons see very little future for themselves in Ethiopia, and they try to hedge against these uncertainties by buying property[33] (because the Ethiopian Birr is expected to depreciate drastically) and opening foreign accounts in foreign banks. This of course is not good for the economy and society.

The economy is controlled by the Pr5 group, and their associates in government. Since the country of about 70 million people is dependent on foreign aid any lowering of the aid flows from the current level would force the Pr5 government to enforce a more onerous taxation on the population, which will differentially treat the citizens, for example, imposing strict taxation on Pr1-Pr4 and sparing or taxing lightly the Pr5. Since all enterprises are bankrupt, the paying capacity of the businesses is zero and of the larger segment of the total population negative.

If the forces in government tried to collect taxes from Pr5, which they must in the absence of foreign aid, because all other taxpayers have lost taxable capacity by government mismanagement, the Pr5 quickly change sides and become a part of the complaining public against the government and supporting change. This opportunistic behavior of PR5 is good for the society. It shows that even Pr5, the last Bastian for the defense of the system, are flexible and are unprepared to blow themselves up together with innocent victims around them. It would be assumed at least the elite or leadership group of the Pr5 is knowledgeable of the above trends and are unlikely to unleash their destructive power on economy and society, by, for example, continued deceptive signaling, which could include

---

[33] The whole area of property rights legislation and protection is in an uncertain state. The care-taker administration of Addis Ababa after the June 2005 elections had to behave cautiously. But the town administration before and after the care-taker administration acted carelessly and recklessly: giving out land and housing permits to favored individuals and groups and denying others public service on the excuse that they had to wait new legislation, directive from government or appointments.

xenophobia, and informing their constituents of eminent danger from majority ethnic and possibly also Moslem groups (Rwanda syndrome!).

Table 1: Typology of Business Behavior

Type*	Description
PR1	These consist of individual businessmen and women with no connection to EPRDF or its associates. They have used their own resources and they know things are not alright: the status of private property rights legislation and protection is not clear and there is fear that their position is looked at with suspicion by government as well as the public. Nevertheless, they persist in doing their duties as citizens and businesspersons; following government rules if they exist and relying on their common sense and education in cases where there are no rules. These act like the Chief Banker under Emperor Haile-Selassie who opened special bank accounts in which he kept money which he owed the Ethiopian Government according to the personal and business income tax proclamation but there was no Government bureaucracy to take the money.
Pr2	consist of individuals who by one or other method acquired wealth (which they believe is inappropriate) in an environment where government cannot carry out its control and regulatory functions but have convinced themselves that the best thing they could do is do good with the wealth like in the Biblical parable and face judgment day
Pr3	These found it impossible to live under the Derg and either went into hiding or left the country but have now returned to resume their lives under freedom. These do not require any special support from government and society except recognition and protection of their human and property rights, for example, the gold smiths in Addis Ababa
Pr4	Argaw before joining the criminal mafia
Pr5	Those who believe they deserve what they got by force of arms. They may have participated directly or indirectly in the alleged criminal activities under EPRDF and never faced prosecution because they control government. Even though their leadership may be aware of its limitation of power, the laity acts as conquerors. For them government is there to rule and they are the government. They are well connected to their membership in government which they use to siphon public resources. They have no aptitude for business, and think they are doing well by destroying the Argaws (genuine entrepreneurs) and corrupting the bureaucracy and its professionals.
*Pr stands for type of private property owners	

There are few if any foreign direct investments from the industrialized market economies. Very little is known about the origin, ownership structure and legal status of the "flower export" business.[34] Even for neo-colonialist operations and foreign mafia businesses, Ethiopia, a basket case, is unattractive.

The vast majority perhaps as many as 80 percent of the total population are in agriculture. The effort to establish property right systems in land over 1942-1975 period was stopped by the Derg and private property rights were abolished. To this day no change is made to the system of collectivist ownership of land. Marxist ideology is replaced by "tribal" ideology and it is causing a worse destruction of property and erosion of social values. The problem which Argaw faced in merchandise retail trade (Box 6) is faced by many farmers wherever they are located.

A conclusion of the above discussion is that sustainable private property development is not possible under the Pr5, which must be looked at as a separable group and differentiated from the government. Secondly, destructive opportunism can be driven in the Ethiopian case by foreign assistance, from governments and groups interested in the destruction of the Ethiopian state and/or by aid, benevolent actions and even FDIs inadvertently carried out without an understanding of how the rulers on the Ethiopian side actually think and work. Thirdly, even if such outside interests with malicious intent existed, they cannot succeed in using PR5 to damage society and economy because Pr5 is a spent force (an evidence of G^4 stranglehold or growing control of the place).

---

[34] The government media often reported production and export of flowers as a major foreign exchange earner in the country – with very little information on ownership, management structure and conditions of work in the industry.

3. Aid and Transaction Costs

On the donor side of aid management are "western" governments and the World Bank and the IMF boards of governors which in the principal-agent theory framework constitute the principal. Working for the principal are the bureaucrats and consultants of the donor organizations which constitute the agent. The bureaucrats and consultants of the donor organization (the agent) can use information asymmetry (they have better information than donors on aid utilization in Ethiopia and how the Ethiopian authorities work) to act opportunistically. Donors (or the principal) are assumed to lack the information which the agent has. In order to ensure that the agent works for the donor, the donor introduces strict or complete contracts, incentives and surveillance, which limit the scope of opportunistic behavior of the agent. If the donors do not speak with one voice (many donor governments and monetary and aid organizations are involved) this introduces another complication on the principal-agent relationship, perhaps giving greater possibilities for opportunistic behavior on the part of the agent.

On the Ethiopian side, the Ethiopian authorities (the agents) are not accountable to the Ethiopian people or parliament (the principal). The agents have virtually controlled government and are outside the purview of the Ethiopian people or parliament. The parliament is captured by the ruling party or government. With government combining the properties of both principal and agent it does not make sense to talk about contracts. The Ethiopian agent-cum-principal acts in unrestricted ways as ruler over a conquered population. This provides the favorable condition for collusion between the agencies and operatives on the donor side with the Ethiopian government operatives for sustained pilferage of aid.

That is one cause for aid ineffectiveness. The solution to this problem can be provided by the donors instituting surveillance, strict (or complete) contracts, regulation, incentives, etc. But that is for problems arising on the donor side of aid management. The problem as argued above is not so much on the donors' side, but it is failure on the Ethiopian side. The Ethiopian side fails to meet its obligations and may deliberately seek ways to take away aid money for personal use. *There is no solution to curving the problem on the Ethiopian side other than establishment of a good-governance government in Ethiopia.*

Aid is like medicine. If the medicine is handled by a competent physician it is curative. But if it is wrongly used it can be fatal. This parable can be decoded into a realistic story on aid. Let us assume the XHS aid is US$ 200 million to house 5000 families. If it did not reach pre-identified and registered 5000 slum dwellers, the cost to society is infinite. How come? It is shown that the project implementing authority would require infinite amount of resources to prove that it is the slum dwellers that are occupying the building using deceptive signaling (transaction cost theorem). Because the true slum dwellers are evicted from their place in order to make room for the apartment building, they have suffered physical and psychological damage in the hands of the authorities. Society around them is agonized by a sense of collective guilt (in the sense that it could not do anything to alleviate the suffering of the evicted households) and outrage at the misdeeds and injustices of the authorities. The 5000 that actually occupied the building have to lie for the rest of their lives, or sell and go somewhere else to lead a pretentious life. If they chose to stay in the XHS building, the authorities have to deploy armed guards in order to protect the 5000 families that by default occupied the XHS building. These guards cannot be police college graduates. They are probably tribal loyalists or criminally bent recruits who lack the consciousness of living under the Ten Commandments.[35] There is no number beyond infinity. Thus, a US$ 200 million in aid gives rise to a social cost or transaction cost of infinity.

---

[35] There is a widespread practice of using military and police personnel from minority peoples, nations and nationalities, and from "outside states' to signal "democracy" (for the international community) as well as threat and intimidation for locals. Often these recruits are poorly trained and while the government secures their loyalty (or believes it secures their loyalties) by giving them employment and a chance to intimidate their former alleged oppressors, it is trying to tell the "captured population" that they are under its mercy: it can unleash this people who are not from the rulers' (or government) tribal base; and if the international community persisted for disclosure of police brutality and crimes like that, government would then try to show that the perpetrators are not from the ruling ethnic group. As a matter of fact the EPRDF has used to great effect this deceitful signaling first to draw into government the Oromo Liberation Front and later to oust it from government and regain the acknowledgement and support of the non-Oromo population (more or less for the ruling ethnic rulers to posture as "saviors" of the non-Oromo population). The whites in South Africa have used coloreds and immigrant Africans during the apartheid era to intimidate and persecute indigenous South Africans.

If the XHS is aware of the true value of their aid, they figure that the transaction cost can be reduced by withholding aid. By so doing they reduce the potential damage of the aid. If transaction cost generated by the 200 million Dollars is infinity, can't we say the damage is done already and it cannot be undone? The authorities that implemented the housing project are restricted by the damage they can inflict on society. They need money to cloth, arm and pay their mercenaries that cannot be regarded by the larger society as one of their own. It could happen as it did in the times of the Derg, when the Derg lost capacity to pay its large army, that army chose to disband, or fall upon itself rather than kill its own people. The present authorities could face a similar situation, when a government force, all of a sudden changes its allegiance and submits to the will of the people and choose to pay a heavy price to do that. The society in the meanwhile unable to feed itself and too dependent on aid grows desperate by the day, and the authorities increasingly becoming unable to contain the anger and frustration of the people. Therefore, it is only if XHS gave another 200 million Dollars to the implementing authorities that they could be accused of funding deceptive signaling and fanning transaction costs.

Can the 200 million Dollar aid yield infinite benefits, just like it can generate infinite transaction costs? The answer is yes; that is how the Germans and the Japanese rose from the ashes during the early part of the post-World War II years. First, they took stock of their assets, very little beyond human capital. They applied their collective ingenuity to preserve and make good use of this scarce resource. The fact that the Japanese are Buddhists and the Germans Christians shows that the Ten Commandments are universal tenets of all religions that guide all human beings to happiness and spiritual contentment. Second, in the doing of things it is important to determine where things have to go: the housing to the predetermined 5000 slum dwellers, the investment capital to the Argaws (or entrepreneurs), construction engineering to construction engineers, the church services to clergy, school administration to graduates of educational administration, nuclear research to the nuclear scientist, etc.[36] Third, and perhaps most important, both the Germans and Japanese were able to create the conditions for the maintenance and effective use of their

---

[36] This is what the Ethiopian administration under emperor Haile-Selassie attempted to do with Western donors and advisors: expand all levels of modern education and professionalize the bureaucracy.

human capital – the most decisive force in development. It is not pecuniary incentives that was used but the healthy environment created by a good-governance government which gave them recognition, challenge and serving their fellow humans in peace and freedom. Most of them chose to stay and work for less because they were rewarded by love and contentment. Things like armed guards, police, navy, air force are necessary to defend territorial integrity and confront domestic criminals. Nothing could stop the Soviets and the Allies from occupying Germany after the suicide of Hitler and after the nuclear bombing of Hiroshima and Nagasaki in Japan. There was no need to have men under arms for a defeated country. As for the local criminal, with all the caring and moral sanctions of a society determined to succeed, it must be a sick criminal to want to harm society. The society ensured that nobody could benefit from a criminal act. 200 million Dollars extra can be a help to the receiver and a psychological comfort for the donor who can now, for such a small price, be a part of human success of epic proportions.

Hence, the aid derivatives of the transaction cost theorem.

1st derivative of the transaction cost theorem:

> *Foreign aid could result in a transaction cost of infinity if deceptive signals are used; and it can yield infinite benefits when honest signals are used under conditions of good-governance government.*

A reformulation of the first derivative:

> *Much more than the direct benefits of aid, it is the negative fallout from the aid that is debilitating society and economy.*

There is positive fallout from aid, but that is achievable only under good-governance government (see discussion on "infinite benefits" from the early post-war year's experience of Germany and Japan). One may perhaps argue that it should not matter which 5000 among millions of slum dwellers should be housed first, any 5000 slum-dwellers would do. It is the fallout from an initial mistake or wrongdoing that society is adversely affected by. The anger and the frustration of the deserving 5000 is magnified by an entire society of people who could not accept the injustices and wrongdoings of those in authority. That is the birth of

39

terrorism. It is a state of affairs where, in the absence of good-governance government, there is no means of peaceful resolution of conflict and the individual decides to correct the wrongs in the society unilaterally and uses any means to do so. Words lose their meaning, when government official talks about law and order, people ask what law and order, whose law and order? There is law and order when and if the XHS building housed not any 5000 slum dwellers but the screened and pre-registered 5000 slum dwellers. When 5000 non-slum dwellers occupy the buildings, the sense of lawlessness and non-orderliness is magnified several fold.

2nd derivative of the transaction cost theorem

> *One can reduce transaction costs for society by withdrawing aid in situations where deceptive signals are used.*

Existing protocols may put some restrictions on what the donor can do. A government of a poor country may claim it has a constitution which gives it the right not to accept aid unless it is a non-conditional aid; or a dictatorial regime may say so without reference to a constitutional limitation because there is no constitution, or the dictator has not read the constitution. Thus, the XHS may give US$ 200 million to the Ethiopian authorities, knowing that the Ethiopians are not under a good-governance government. But if the XHS itself falls under a good-governance government, it is expected to know about the negative fallouts from aid, and know also it is when the time comes for additional aid that it can do something about it. In that event, it is unlikely that the XHS would provide aid for slum dwellers in Addis Ababa unless a good-governance government is established in that country. That is why the new generation of donors of the new world order is imposing the food-aid conditionality:

> *Food aid is unconditional aid, given to all countries and people in need, but development aid is conditional, and is given only to countries that have good-governance government.*

Looked at from the point of view of efficient management of global resources, this conditionality is reasonable. If aid beyond the food-aid threshold is given in the absence of good-governance government, transaction costs rise – the society suffers more than the benefits it could theoretically get from the development aid. Withdrawing the development aid reduces transaction costs.

On the other hand, withdrawing food aid means allowing the population to die. If the authorities want to control the food aid, without establishing themselves as good-governance government, then the authorities are making a criminal mistake. The international community (or G^4) will be forced to fight the authorities and get them to book in order to save the population.

The brave new world has declared that food aid is human right and all the people in the troubled Horn area are entitled to it, even Somalia where there is no government Somalis are entitled to it. The presence of the invisible hand of the invisible *global good-governance government* is revealed in Somalia, where there is no formal government (only warlordism), by the shipment of food aid which is extremely costly to do. Yet, that is the most transaction cost reducing way of delivering food to the Somali people. The global good-governance government is transaction cost reducing.

If the authorities became a good-governance government, then the donors will give both food aid and development aid. In other words, there are literally billions of US Dollars of aid that will flow in to help the Ethiopian people place themselves on a sustainable course of development. More importantly, since sustainable development cannot grow out of aid, there would be FDI inflows when a good-governance government is put in place.

However, just like with democracy, there is a play of words regarding the concept of good-governance government (see section 4). A good-governance government is not something the authorities can claim as they did with "democracy" during the cold-war period. It is what the people and the international community (i.e. the global good-governance government) determine.

3$^{nd.}$ derivative of the transaction cost theorem

> *All aid is not necessarily good aid; aid coming from a non good-governance government source could be transaction cost*

increasing. Any aid from any source given to a non-good-governance government above the food-aid threshold is transaction cost increasing

Thus, the aid Ethiopia received from the Soviet Union was destabilizing and transaction cost producing. Aid coming into Ethiopia from a non-good-governance government source (be it Russia, China, or Saudi Arabia) would not be based on the need to maintain the aid at the level of food-aid threshold. It is established that a Ruble of aid above the food-aid threshold increases transaction costs to infinity. Withdrawal of that aid will be transaction cost decreasing.

We notice that the US Government will never give aid for building churches or mosques in Ethiopia, while most Arab countries are not constrained from doing that. This is because there are no good-governance governments in these Arab countries. There is a good chance that their aid for mosques would go to fund sectarianism and anger the Christians who see that as interference in their internal affairs.[37]

On the other hand, aid coming from a good-governance government source is transaction cost reducing. The US government can only give aid which enhances private property development, either directly to the entrepreneurs (Argaws) if it can or through government conditionally, so that it reaches entrepreneurs indirectly. The USA government aid could go to fund bridges, dams, schools, roads and hospitals (public property development) with a view to enabling recipient governments support private property development in their countries.[38] But, today the aid recipient governments must be good-governance governments in order to qualify for development aid.

That is why Africans and the whole donor community should be weary of Chinese aid to Africa. The Chinese can repeat what the Soviets did at this wrong time and place for them. For example, the Chinese might give aid

---

[37] Ethiopian Christians and Moslems believe in a secular government and that government does not receive aid from G^4 or anybody else for building churches for the Christians.

[38] See Chapter 4 of textbook, where the objective of public policy and public property development is defined as enhancing private property development under good-governance government.

to a dictatorial regime in Africa whose leader and his groomed son to succeed him have been on a spending spree for three or four days and spent the equivalent of perhaps two to three years of foreign aid for a poor African country.[39] This happens because right now the Chinese are not having a good-governance government (no control of the people over government, there is no independence of the judiciary; no freedom of the press, the communist government does not protect private property rights for the Chinese). The ruler and his son is the government of the African country. Any aid to that country could be transaction cost increasing, whether the donor is conscious of it or not.

Chinese aid to Ethiopia cannot be directed at private property development (ideological reasons). It will therefore go directly to Pr5 and their membership in government. It will go to keep the mercenary forces of the regime in luxurious apartment buildings, to pay these forces wages and salaries and give them the firepower to shoot at peaceful demonstrators. It goes to empower the regime to deny internet access to some literate internet using Ethiopians and assist the regime in its adventures toward thought and behavioral control. The police and military of the regime does not protect the slum dwellers evicted from their shacks, it goes against them to protect the impostors who are occupying XHS buildings and Pr5 "businessmen and women". If the Chinese built dams, bridges and roads it belongs to Pr5 and their associates in government. Only they can use them. The rest of the population lives on food-aid.

Therefore, Chinese government aid to Ethiopia through the Ethiopian government, conflicts with the food-aid (or development aid) conditionality. It means the Chinese aid will allow for an astronomical increase of transaction costs and increase the negative fallouts, which will have debilitating effect on economy and society. If the Chinese do not want to do that, then they would be expected to synchronize their aid with the rest of the donor community. As a minimum the Chinese would have helped the Ethiopians if they withheld their aid.

Thus, it can be concluded the Chinese can help the Ethiopian people in anyone or a combination of ways:

---

[39] This episode was disclosed by CNN (7/9/09). It is strange that the disclosure was not done by a French private media or government, or is it not surprising?

1. Withdrawing their aid from reaching a non-good-governance government in Ethiopia is transaction cost reducing (3rd aid derivative of transaction cost theorem)

2. The Chinese can give (helpful) aid to the Ethiopians (even without themselves adopting good-governance government) through the G^4 management coordination (see section 3.3).

3. The Chinese can give (helpful) aid to the Ethiopians (even while they themselves are adopting good-governance government) by collaborating with the management of G^4. For example, they could institute together with the G^4 management protocols, global systems (organizations) and surveillance mechanisms to prevent Chinese businesses and individuals from establishing *neo-colonialist* relations[40] with rulers and interest groups in countries like Ethiopia which don't have good-governance governments. This is in addition to the aid they can give directly based on the food-aid conditionality. They can also institute measures coordinated with the G^4 management to limit capital flight from Africa through fraudulent trade (under-invoicing of exports and over-invoicing imports) and by dictatorial rulers of African countries.

3.1 Property Development and Acceleration of Transaction Cost Growth

Suppose we have, not one but two XHS equal housing projects (XHS I and II). It can be concluded that the negative fallouts would double as *a minimum* – 10,000 instead of 5000 evicted households or households that have not been screened and pre-registered. There are then an equivalent number of households, actual occupants of the XHS building, who lie or

---

[40] A neocolonialist relation is a system of prolongation of the exploitative colonialist relations (direct rule by the colonizer) through an alliance between the former colonizer and the native rulers. To many students of economics and history, neocolonialism is perhaps a more exploitative and degrading form of social and economic relations.

disguise themselves from society. These true beneficiaries are not expected to advertise themselves in front of the camera for the benefits of the authorities and give proof that they are the 5000 or 10,000 pre-registered slum dwellers who are now housed in the XHS project. Unless they are the true screened and pre-registered slum dwellers, they are not going to testify that their association worked with XHS, civil society organizations (banned by the government) and the bureaucracy to complete the XHS project.

Unlike the impostors the true slum dwellers would like to have visibility, form slum dwellers associations and would wish to work with civil society organizations, the free media and with government. The impostors, on the other hand, will work with government to prevent free associations from forming and do everything in their power to prevent the disclosure of the truth about them and how they got the XHS apartment.

The impostors require the complete elimination of all the people who know the truth about their occupation of the XHS building, but that is too costly and is impossible to achieve. The only way of solving this problem most cheaply is for these people to come forward with the truth. This helps clean the soul, saves their descendents from paying a heavy price to remove their guilt by association (which must at some stage include revelation of the truth about the misdeeds of their forebears long ago dead), and importantly, create a condition for the cooperation between them and the true slum dwellers so that both groups and many others like them can be properly housed. Society draws pleasure, inspiration and hope from this cooperation.

In the mean while, the authority that negotiated with XHS, the donor agency for the slum dwellers housing project, may go on with deceptive signaling to protect the impostors. It tries to do that, for example, by abolishing the free press, closing offices of the political opposition and the civil society, by trying to establish parallel government institutions to replace these, and by destroying the bureaucracy and manning it by Boxer types of bureaucrats, since Type 1-3 bureaucrats will not cooperate to lie (use deceptive signaling) in public. Not only the authority does not succeed but it also requires resources, infinite amount of resources, all to prove the impossible: that the true slum dwellers are the actual occupants of the XHS building.

The chances are the negative fallouts from the two XHS projects will be more than twice the negative fallout from one XHS housing project. What it means is with every additional development project (apartment building, a public enterprise, a dam, road construction, etc.) the negative fallouts keep on cumulating. At the same time the capacity of government to reduce or limit transaction costs remains the same or declines. In this case the likely occurrence is a problem-solving capacity decline. Once the bureaucracy is corrupted in one department there is a good chance that the practice spreads quickly engulfing the whole governance system. Information and rumors also spread like wild fire informing people about the misdeeds of government and about the excesses of those groups that corrupt government.

This becomes a reiteration of the second aid derivative of the transaction cost theorem. Any private enterprise or public enterprise (worse!) added to the Ethiopian economy generates infinite times (a meaningless number) more negative fallouts than the benefits from the face value of the investment. Once the enterprise is established, closing it becomes a transaction cost reducing measure. That is why Africans talk of their natural resources as curses, simply because the exploitation of the resources brings more social cost than benefits.

3.2 Individual Rational Responses to the Absence of Good-Governance Government

The link between aid or any investment expenditures and the existence of the *global good-governance government* can be analyzed from observed market and government behavior.

1. Suppose Argaw's rich son, living and working in the United States, gave his father US$ 4 million. Argaw knows that money is an extremely precious scarce resource. He could not invest it productively in Ethiopia, where the ruler of the state of peoples, nations and nationalities and the criminals in his police force together with their followers in society would rob him or (worse) arrange to have him killed in some accident if that is the better way of taking the money from him. Argaw, Ethiopia's hope, will advise

his son to invest the money in the USA where it could have positive rates of return and send him the yield in small installments so that he can try to live in the country he loves with clear conscience and inconspicuously. Any time Argaw shows an improved lifestyle the ruler of the peoples, nations and nationalities or any of his cronies will rob him. The show of wealth will be the cause of death and not the index of recognition or of labor productivity as in the Coasean world. This is the problem faced by all Pr1 in trying to live and work in Ethiopia. They all have two choices: leave the country; or if they decided to stay they should live a life close to the food aid recipient.

2. The goldsmiths in Addis Ababa have no better option. Their best hope would be if American, European and Japanese tourists were to visit. But the USA Government would advise its citizens not to visit: they will be attacked by terrorists who blame the US Government for helping the Ethiopian regime. They can also be robbed (or worse) by the gang organized under the rule of peoples, nations and nationalities. Pr5 will buy the jewels but these do not provide a sustainable market for the jeweler. The rest of the population, i.e. the vast majority, lives under a regime of food-aid. The goldsmiths too have either to leave the country, or stay under the protection of armed guards and face the wrath of the people on judgment day or share what they have with the people. The last option may give them spiritual satisfaction (as Beletu did), but the Pr5 rulers may not like it.

3. How about other entrepreneurs who are not Pr5 members? These may build tall buildings, luxurious villas, establish banks, do commerce, etc. With these activities, they prove to the economics student that they are not good Coasean "entrepreneurial coordinators", because they are investing in activities with negative rates of return. If they borrowed money from the bank to carry out their investment, the Pr5 government will go after them and confiscate their property, which will not be useful for government either.

4. Pr5 "impostors" may own tall buildings, drive 4W vehicles, arrange for their buildings to be rented by government

departments, and live well. But all this becomes a waiting game, while the wrath of the impoverished people around them continues to grow and their mercenary forces that keep them protected threaten to rebel. These mercenary forces would eventually rebel as they did under the Derg when the Pr5 government fails to pay them. The Pr5 rulers may know, but the laity may not know that donor money cannot go to pay the military of Pr5. The rulers may want to tax the people, but then the people have lost their taxable capacity through misrule. Just like the Derg's military falling upon itself the Pr5 military will eventually face the choice of destroying itself together with the defenseless people (warlordism in Somalia), or muster the courage and submit to the will of the people. The Derg's over a million men army had strong leadership and chose this option, and by so doing they perhaps won the forgiveness, affection and appreciation of the Ethiopian people. The Pr5 regime today holds public debate intended to misinform not the Ethiopian people, because they know, but the international community that it is their military which has liberated the people from the Derg military.[41] Using deceptive signaling, government may require infinite resources which, even if the government were to have it, it will not be able to prove the impossible.

5. What about the regional public enterprises and the federal government public enterprises? Whether these are kept in one or evenly distributed in all states they are bankrupt businesses. One reduces transaction costs by closing them and keeping them open becomes a drain on the treasury. The options for society in dealing with the public enterprises have been discussed.

6. Foreign direct investment from western market economies is unlikely, because their western governments and investment

---

[41] Imagine the Americans and the British (and others who cooperated with them) who arranged for the EPRDF government to be installed in Ethiopia receiving a lecture from its Boxer type leaders on how the EPRDF defeated the Derg military and liberated the Ethiopian "peoples". When the leadership does this are they trying to misinform the world, knowing that the British and the Americans whom they consider to be their allies will not tell the truth? In the meanwhile, the invisible good-governance government (which the Americans and the British are not claiming but which is revealing itself by some of the major happenings in the world today) has successfully reduced the EPRDF government to a one-man rule.

consultants will advise them not to invest in Ethiopia due to political and other risks. Mafia type business operatives, especially from less regulated places such as South and East Asia are a possibility. But these go to places like Congo, Nigeria, Sudan, Angola, etc. where the opportunities to steal and live by crime through the creation of collaborative ventures with local rulers exist. The only resource to steal in Ethiopia is aid and that is controlled by donor or the global good-governance government which the donor serves.

3.3 The Role of the Donor

The invisible global good-governance government or the donor working for it knows that any development aid it tries to channel over and above the food-aid threshold through the EPRDF only increases transaction costs. Therefore, it will impose the food aid conditionality. Unlike in the Soviet years, the donor also tries to protect the people from a Rwanda type of conflagrations by helping the government or regime if it is moving in the direction of good-governance government and by limiting its capacity to damage society if the regime chose the opposite path.

Therefore, understanding the role of the donor and the global good-governance government which it serves is key to survive or prevail in the new globalized economy. The donor, representing the invisible global good-governance government, helps by educating the Ethiopian people and their government about the nature and structure of a good-governance government and how it works. If the Ethiopian government is a "good student" and follows the donor's instructions then there will be development aid over and above food aid coming into the country. As incentives to the government and also to encourage the people to persevere, not to lose hope and not to start terrorism (like sending revolutionary martyrs to blow themselves up with innocent victims around them), the donor allows some wastage of aid resources.

For example, even as the government destroyed the bureaucracy, aid money flows into the Business Process Reengineering (BPR) Program which the donor finances. The donor knows (information asymmetry) it does not help improve the bureaucracy, but it may allow some money to

49

reach the true professional survivors in the country. As we saw in Ethiopia, the rulers and their professionals shared that money with a dwindling number of true professionals still alive and in the country. Donor money may flow in to fund discussions to introduce "modular systems" of educational management, to train students in "competition policy", or to devise post-graduate programs. Regarding the training, explanation is already given as to its worth. Concerning, the modular system or designing post-graduate degree programs one observes a gathering of people to "reinvent the wheel". If one is interested in the money paid for attendance or does not want to risk sanctions or even expulsion, then one does not ask questions such as "who is ordering this work (i.e. the PBR, the post-graduate program or modular system) to be carried out?", "where does the finance for this come from?" "How about the work rules and the legally established institutions in charge of these activities?", "what happened to professionals in curriculum design, educational administration, etc. and why are we having this committee of physics professors, mathematicians, botanists, microbiologists, etc. to sit on the podium and lead the discussions?" "If the committee members say they don't own the program, who does?"

The problem for the donor soon becomes how to reach the true professional and keep him/her alive and physically comfortable (because the spirit is being tortured) still through a working arrangement with the regime which now works to frustrate both the donor and the true professional from achieving their objectives. Among the ways of reaching the true professional practiced by the donor is organizing individual targeting prizes, strict or more complete contracts negotiated with the government, establishing NGOs to be headed by true professionals, etc.

It is not difficult to notice that the whole activity is managed by a union of type 1 bureaucrats and boxer type institution heads. These, especially the type 1 bureaucrats, do not appear on the proceedings. The Boxer type may appear before the camera believing that he is doing his duty and helping in the realization of the goal of the program. This individual usually suppresses information concerning the source of the fund and the conditions under which it is received. Instead, he uses the occasion to tell how his government is changing things and correcting the mistakes of the past. Whether or not the movers are cognizant of the donor's knowledge about them is hard to tell. It is also hard to tell if the donors' agents themselves are cognizant of the knowledge about them of the invisible global good-governance government or the principal they serve.

Rules are made by committees; parliament is ignored and structured to serve as a rubberstamp of the government. Parliament is also used for sending deceptive signals that parliamentary democracy is practiced in Ethiopia. There is no high government official except Boxer type (indicator of government inability to recruit qualified personnel) to take responsibility and own the program. Clearly there is no rule of law in that society. Global good-governance government, which controls the aid, reveals its existence by the fact that society is shielded from rule by warlords, or society did not suffer yet Rwanda type of social and economic upheavals and crises, and government is continuously assisted to change its ways.

Still no harm is done, it is the donor's money and only the manager of global resources (global good-governance government) should be concerned about this waste. How long the Ethiopian people should persevere and how long is this balancing act by the donor or the invisible good governance government maintained? These are the pertinent questions of our time.

Understanding the nature and evolution of the invisible global good-governance government is difficult, but all that the student of economics can do is show and analyze its various manifestations. Per capita income fails to indicate the growth of problem-solving capacity. When properties are added to the fray, they generate multiple problems and the easiest method of solving the problems, from the perspective of non-good-governance governments[42] is eliminating them from the source: killing the source, closing the civil society organization, banning the free press, using deceptive signaling to great effect, etc. These are all demonstrated destructively opportunistic behaviors discussed in this monograph which are carried out consciously or without the realization of the consequences of measures taken (the Boxer story). All these are destructive methods, they cannot eliminate the problems. As a matter of fact, they make the problems "hibernate" and multiply only to resurge with far greater ferocity than when they initially emerged. In the end they destroy economy and

---

[42] These include theocracies, ethnocracies, and dictatorships of all forms and descriptions.

society and drag back civilization to a state where even the little progress society made before these regimes took over is lost. It took almost 80 years of Soviet rule, and in the end Russia returned to where the Soviet Union was in 1917 (back to the drawing board). The only correct way of solving problems of development is via good-governance government. That avoids relapses and makes it possible for society to progress continuously on incremental basis. However, that requires the conversion (or reincarnation) of the invisible good-governance government into the visible good-governance government.

3.4 The Advantages of the Aid Dependent Economy for a Major Breakthrough

The absence of good-governance government has been introduced as a major constraint on development. In order to facilitate an understanding of the concept of the invisible global good-governance government (G^4) consider its differences and similarities with religion. G^4 can be looked at as a man-made "religion" or ideology. Unlike the divine religion which requires a self-contained holy book, prophet and clergy to interpret it to the laity, and the laity for whom it is written, G^4 consists of an incomplete written text (to be revised and changed), which means its content across time is not constant but variable. G^4 does not require prophet or clergy to interpret, because it is a manmade religion. The ordinary man for whom and by whom it is written is supposed to know and understand it without the need for any intermediation.

If G^4 is invisible and not fully written how can the ordinary man recognize it? The ordinary man recognizes it not by revelation (as in the case of holy books), but by the way it manifests itself. The existence of G^4 is manifested in many ways in the world today, for example, in the G-8, G-20, the General Assembly of the United Nations, the Security Council, the WTO, the *meeting* of the Chinese and US authorities, the NATO-Russian or the USA-Russian Summits, the meeting of the ministers of finance of the G-20, etc. In the 2009 G-20 meeting in Pittsburgh (USA) the three leaders of the USA, Britain and France took the podium to condemn Iran's secret weapon development, without uttering a word about G^4. One possible reason would be G^4 being a manmade religion they perhaps did not want to complicate matters by acting as interpreters of that pseudo-religion. In these instances G^4 could be regarded as a pseudo-religion or ideology, a rallying point for those in meeting.

There are also dramatic occurrences which are observed manifestations of G^4 as an organization or a system of governance. Thus, the "unofficial" management of G^4 bombs the Afghans, or Iraqis to submit to the common man's religion; organizes sanctions demanding the same of the North Koreans and Iranians; and it threatens with stationing nuclear rocket systems in Poland and Czech Republic to force the Russian acceptance of the religion of good-governance government. One also observes the bombing of the Taliban in Afghanistan and Pakistan while allowing them to create havoc in Somalia; and in Ethiopia cajoling aspirants, both EPRDF and opposition parties, as they are vying for the nonexistent posts of prophet or clergy in the layman's religion. In the case of the Chinese, they are showered with all the technological transfers and industrial relocations that humanity can muster so that they can practice good-governance government and be on a sustainable course of private property development. The invisible global good-governance government watches the Venezuelan leader spending billions of dollars on armaments purchased from Russia and China in order to protect his poor people. In the current (2009) proceedings of the UN General Assembly some heads of states and government were articulating the content of the incomplete ever changing and unholy book that is G^4, without ever mentioning it by name. Thus, there are many ways the people of this planet are forced to being converts of the manmade religion and becoming both the prophet and cleric of that religion.

Let us review some of the various materialization or reincarnation problems of G^4. One may think of the USA or the rulers of the USA as being G^4 or followers of G^4, but they are neither. We observe the US Congress debating whether or not to send more troops and spend more money in Afghanistan, as they are bombing the place. If they knew why they are there in the first place, this matter should not be debated now. Withdrawal from Afghanistan cannot be an option for the USA unless defeated in battle. If they withdrew the Rwanda situation may resurge under the victorious Taliban; and the Americans, their allies and their future descendents must then be prepared to carry collective guilt forever – because they cannot say as their forebears did they did not know.

If the government of the USA cannot agree to uphold the religion or gospel of G^4 and explain with it its presence and involvement in Afghanistan, Pakistan, Iraq, Iran, Ethiopia, Somalia, Djibouti, Eritrea, Myanmar, Colombia, Kenya, Korea, Zimbabwe, Mexico, the Middle East, the Balkans, etc. how is it possible to justify all these by a consortium of a group of allied countries?

Including China and Russia to cooperate with the USA without this countries being "baptized" G^4 in the first place becomes problematic. China and Russia may say they agreed or did not agree with the US for a variety of different reasons, but having or knowing what it is they agreed or did not agree with is central for the sustenance of that cooperative relationship. If the "gospel" of G^4 is the basis of the cooperation, then the Chinese authorities would be expected to be cognizant that a Yuan of aid they give to Ethiopia, in the absence of good-governance government in Ethiopia, above the food-aid threshold, will inflict more damage (increase transaction costs) on the Ethiopian people than benefit them. They would help the Ethiopian people by withholding their aid (the incontrovertible evidence is provided). In other words, the Chinese themselves need not embrace G^4 in order to help Ethiopians by withdrawing their aid. To withdraw their aid and help Ethiopians by doing so all they have to do is see the evidence of the destructiveness of that aid, when given beyond and above the food-aid threshold.

More importantly, the Chinese must themselves embrace G^4. Private property development (the economic goals of all societies and which the Chinese are having with FDI, industrial relocation and technological transfers) will not be sustainable, unless China embraced the manmade pseudo-religion of good-governance government.[43] The G^4 management

---

[43] In order to understand this compelling justification for the Chinese expected embrace of G^4, note that the Rubicon was crossed in China-West relations when the West did two things: (i) the West unilaterally inundated China with technology, industrial relocation and capacity building without seeking anything in return from China, so that China became in a short period of time a member of the top 5 world's largest industrial goods producers. (ii) The West based on their experience informed the

has sent honest signals to the Chinese: sustainable private property development is not possible under a collectivist system of economic management, if it were so the Soviets would still have been in power in Russia.

By withholding their aid, the Russians are in fact helping the Ethiopian people.[44] But, what is being said in addition is that for both China and

---

Chinese (sent honest signals) that private property development (which the Chinese now acquired) is not sustainable without embracing good-governance government. As a result China today does not need its industrial espionage network, the manufacture of nuclear weapons because the perceived dangers have been removed. What the West gave the Chinese are private properties not collective properties. What the West promised to give the Chinese is the knowledge of how to manage and develop private properties. The Chinese acceptance of both "free gifts" is key to China's success and determines whether or not China is going to have a place in the driver's seat of global change.

China and Russia today do not have to wait until they are converted to G^4 first before they participate with G^4 management in global problem solving (the sequencing problem). They can join right away in the writing of the latest version of the pseudo-religion (G^4), in the establishment of its governance structure (e.g. WTO, UN General Assembly, Security Council, World Intellectual Property Organization (WIPO), International Labour Organization (ILO), etc.), in enforcing a G^4 plan for aid-dependent economy such as Ethiopia and in fast-trucking their own G^4 transformation or reincarnation.

There is now incontrovertible evidence that the two central propositions in this discussion are true, namely (a) that sustainable private property development is possible only under good-governance government, and (b) a Yuan of aid given to Ethiopia above the food-aid threshold today generates more cost than benefit. The proof for (b) is dealt with in this monograph, and that of (a) is provided in the forthcoming textbook on the *Economics of Private Property Development*, which is summarized in section 4 of this monograph. (c) China could help Ethiopia by withholding aid to the Ethiopian government; but China can also help Ethiopia by cooperating and synchronizing its aid with G^4 management. Thus, whereas the Soviet contribution to human salvation and progress is over, Chinese contribution in that direction is only beginning.

[44] The Soviets were giving the aid the Chinese may want to give to poor countries today. The Soviet aid to the liberation movements in the three continents achieved its aims; but the soviet aid to independent countries such as Ethiopia had been destabilizing. The Soviet aid to the liberation struggle represented the sacrifices made by people, the Soviet people, in order to save humanity from colonialism and neo-colonialism. The

Russia, it is not possible to have sustainable private property development in their respective countries without themselves embracing good-governance government.

The Russians of today have two choices: keep the banner of the Soviets and lead in the struggle for human liberation and freedom, equality and justice; or take the place of the colonialist and the neo-colonialist. If they chose the latter, any military aid they give to Ethiopia must be to harm or damage the Ethiopian People. Any Ruble they give as aid to the Ethiopians over and above the food-aid threshold will frustrate the reform program which the G^4 management has in store for Ethiopia and translate into greater cost than benefit the Ethiopians.[45] Although it is not known

---

Soviet citizens, instead of living the luxurious and wasteful life of the colonialist and neo-colonialist chose instead to share the little they have with the victims of that naked barbarism. Had the Soviets not made those sacrifices the helpless Africans, Latin Americans and Asians would have remained inhabitants of a big "reserve" for the expansion of the colonialists and neo-colonialists – to be used when their labour is needed and culled or discarded when the rulers needed more space. The Soviets could have acted like the terrorists today – they had the most powerful destructive war weapons in unsurpassed stocks, capable to blow planet earth and many planets like earth into smithereens together with themselves. But they were followers of a manmade rational "religion" – Marxism Leninism. They knew their mission and once accomplished left for succeeding generations of humans to continue with the next stage of human struggle. The Soviets did not live for Russians or even the Soviets, they lived for humanity.

It is important to note that the Soviet aid to Ethiopia had been destabilizing: generated more harm (increased transaction costs) than benefit the Ethiopian people. Had the Soviet government been a good-governance government, it would have realised the significance of this and would have adopted the aid conditionality. We cannot say that it is because the Russians have realized the significance of the food aid conditionality for not providing aid to Ethiopia at this time. But what we can say is unless and until the Russians embrace good-governance government, they cannot bring about a state of sustainable private property development in Russia, and they cannot help but harm the Ethiopians with their aid.

[45] Since the early 1940s the management of G^4 were actively engaged in supporting the economic, political and social development of the Ethiopian state. The Swedes and the Germans have been helping the Ethiopians to this day, always careful that their aid is directed to the people. The Americans and the British have tried to do likewise by working with both the people and government (hoping in the process to be able to convert the government into a good-governance government). During the past 30 years the USA has been home for about 2 million Ethiopians who escaped certain death under the Derg and from persecutions by the EPRDF regime. Large numbers of

whether or not withdrawal of Russian aid to Ethiopia is as a result of the negative outcomes of Soviet aid, Russian withdrawal of aid is transaction cost reducing for Ethiopia (3rd derivative of the transaction cost theorem). If the Russians and Chinese gave aid above the food-aid threshold, they would have in effect taken the place of the colonialists and neo-colonialists and without the ability to enforce their will because the former colonialists and neo-colonialists have now chosen to work for the benefit of humanity.

Russia must take the first option, which means adopt G^4 and ease the burden of endless sacrifice from the yolk of the Russian people and at the same time continue helping Ethiopians and all humanity as indeed the Soviets had done in the past. There will then be a good basis for a sustainable cooperation between former west and former east, and all humanity will gain from this cooperation.

This cooperation of the West with Russia and China is most efficient, i.e. goal achieving in a consistent and sustainable way only when the latter embrace G^4. First, China and Russia will be assisted by the west in their transformation into a good-governance government regime. Second, China and Russia will become prime movers in solving problems in all theatres of conflict in the World today rather than play the role of the "spoiler" or the "man on the fence" or pause as the defender of the Taliban, supporter of nuclear proliferation, etc. without being effective in the role they are assuming. In other words, Russia and/or China cannot stop human progress today, but by embracing G^4, they would be able to develop both socially and economically, and also contribute to human progress by placing themselves at the centre of the struggle.

Cooperation does not mean being dictated by the USA and its allies. The USA and its allies are not (or have not accepted the position of) the true G^4 or proponent of G^4. For one thing, the "gospel" of G^4 is not completely written, it being an evolving unholy book in which China and

---

"educated Ethiopians" have survived in a number of Western Democracies. The Americans and the British negotiated with the Soviets, the Derg as well as the desperate groups in opposition for a political soft-landing in Ethiopia. They succeeded to have the Soviets leave the place, for the Derg military to disband and for a desperate group in the opposition to assume political power in Ethiopia. They also provided food and a sense of security to the people.

Russia have as much right as anybody else to write in the additional script. It is true Russia and China need to do a lot more in order to change course, while the USA and its allies have only to concern themselves with the incremental changes to make. Even though the USA and its allies have incurred costs to reach where they are today, they are prepared to share their experience and knowledge for free, so that Russia and China as well as Ethiopia and Somalia can cross the greater hurdle of transition. In the case of Ethiopia and Somalia the USA and its allies are even saying they want to cover the costs of transition and seek the cooperation (and if they are willing to give the support) of Russia and China so that they could reduce the cost of doing it. It is a win-win situation for everybody, Russia, China and the whole of humanity included.

In the meanwhile let us review the problems faced by the G^4 management in their effort to convert the Ethiopians to the "new religion" and assist them in establishing, for the first time in their long history, a good-governance government. Despite the extensive commitment (or manifestations of commitment) by the USA and its allies to the wellbeing of the Ethiopian people, it is difficult to be certain about the true position of the USA and its allies. Deceptive signaling complicates the transition into good-governance government. In this adventure, the West is as vulnerable to the statistical probability of failure as to the probability of success so long as there exist information asymmetry.

Information asymmetry, which we used to analyze market behavior in Ethiopia, invariably results in moral hazard and adverse selection. Let us examine Box 7 to see the import of this proposition.

Box 7: Can the End Justify the Means?

During the US Congress debate of early August 2009 on whether or not to continue sending more troops to Afghanistan and increase public expenditures for the war, the war veteran and congressman McCain read out his expected support for a continued engagement until victory. Imagine someone from a price committee in economics calling Mr. McCain and informing him that he won a price for his contribution to transaction cost economics, citing his congress speech which proves that his option is transaction cost reducing. For the sake of demonstrating a point let us assume there is a McCainB and consider these two responses to the award:

McCainB: "Gee! I did? Thanks"

> True McCain: "what did you say I won? Are you sure it is me? Who are you again?" He then proceeds to use government service, and if it is not forthcoming any time soon, use his own personal resources to get at the bottom of this "joker".

In this example, the truth of the matter is Mr. McCain has contributed to transaction cost economics. The alternative to continued war or defeat in battle is the Rwanda type genocide under the Taliban; which in addition to the crises in Afghanistan the whole American nation and its G^4 allies will be forced to live under collective guilt for generations to come. What makes Americans lucky to have the true McCain is that he refuses to accept rewards for something he did not do, even if others believe he did it.

For some people the "end justifies the means", for the true McCain not, because ethics is important. McCain's assumed rejection of the price award was based on the fact that he did not justify continuation of the war because it was transaction cost reducing. Would Mr. McCain accept the prize award if it was based on acknowledgement of his years of service in the US Congress and defending the poor of Afghanistan? This is an aspect of the problem of using deceptive signaling. It allows the signaler to send confusing message and the liberty to make convenient interpretation of it. In this case McCain forces the signaler to transmit honest signals, and by so doing serve and protect society.

Box 7 introduces an aspect of moral hazard inherent in the G^4 proposition, but there are many aspects to this. Some would say "honest signals" are the hallmarks of a good-governance government. But their use becomes target achieving if the signal recipient cannot misinterpret them.

Let us assume the entire Taliban assembled, all in arms and some explosive tied to their bodies, and the joker in Box 7 were to represent G^4 and explain his case to the gathering:

Joker (adopting honest signaling): "Look guys, we (believers in G^4) are bombing you so that you accept global good-governance government, because it is transaction cost minimizing."

How many Taliban are prepared to learn economics and calculus and go through joker's procedures and in the end (20 years later still standing at the place where they assembled in combat gear!) breathe a sigh of relief: "why don't you say so?" How many Taliban are prepared to go with joker because they are impressed by the equations, figures and text material they could not understand; and how many Taliban would say, "I thought I was fighting the agent of the devil, I did not know I am fighting the devil himself" and proceed to action, i.e. blow themselves up together with joker? True McCain would perhaps not agree to the representation of G^4 by joker, and not agree also that the war was for the establishment of good-governance government in Afghanistan.

The difference is this: the Afghans had to adopt G^4 while being bombed. Ethiopians on the other hand are in a situation where they are made to know they will be bombed if they don't accept G^4. One can see establishing good-governance government in Afghanistan is costlier than establishing it in Ethiopia where management of G^4 has a better control of things.[46] In the Ethiopian case G^4 has placed both the government and the political opposition in the country under its control and in such a way that either of them could inflict least damage or no damage at all on the people. In addition, G^4 gives to the population "uncertain" protection, food and a signal that more would come if they could install a good-

---

[46] The Afghanistan war must be won and is costlier than the Ethiopian case. The Sudanese case too is more difficult because the Sudanese government can use its oil proceeds and maintain the stranglehold on the people through purchase of arms from China and/or Russia. G^4 has to make the difficult negotiations with Russia and China to stop the flow of arms in addition to finding transaction cost reducing ways to manage the Sudanese government and its political opposition. The Chinese theatre has been contained by crossing the Rubicon by inundating China with industrial capacity and technology, and signaling the Chinese in no uncertain terms that their economic development cannot be sustainable without converting their rule into a good-governance government regime. The Russians do not have the leverage of the USSR, and the Soviets having accomplished their global mission of liberating man from colonialism and neocolonialism have left succeeding generations of Russians to find their ways to stay at the helm. There too the Rubicon is crossed, the only way to progress for Russia and maintain their leadership position as in Soviet days is to embrace the new rational "religion"- adopt good-governance government, and do so by cooperating with those that have made progress in the establishment of good-governance government.

governance government with its help.[47] G^4 grants the people also the time to see the proof of the proposition that no development (private property development) is possible without good-governance government.

The G^4 management control of Ethiopia goes beyond these and includes its stranglehold on the whole region of the Horn area of Africa. One of the ways of the G^4's manifestation of control of the region is the obstacles it placed for the establishment of independent governments in the region. It is impossible to have a government in Addis Ababa which would abandon its duty to fight for the regaining of the country's costal territories. By creating a situation where the society is divided territorially and politically G^4 management has also made it impossible for the Eritrean and Ethiopian rulers to manage in both Eritrea and Ethiopia. On the other hand, by establishing a NATO base in Djibouti, G^4 management has not only created difficulties for any government in Addis Ababa, it has also further tightened its control of the region and contained the excesses of pan-Arabic ambition to isolate Ethiopia. But, where all these control of the region leads too is unclear.

Very little is known as to whether the apparent acceptance of G^4 management of the system of "peoples, nations and nationalities" arises from its strategic pursuit of stranglehold of the place or it is an adverse policy selection resulting from agent misinformation. Nevertheless, the system lacks economic, political or social justifications. It is effectively used in deceptive signaling, denials and gross violations of human and property rights. The system has also become a major source of aid pilferage. With the donor indicating decision to fund regional or state activities (in the guise of supporting decentralization of government), large portion of aid money are reported missing. The same group controlling the federal government also controls the regional administrations, and when donor complaints about missing funds reach the federal authorities, their readymade answer is non-interference in state affairs and argue that failure on the part of the donor to develop capacity at state level first is the cause of disappearance of aid money.

---

[47] In fact that was already put into effect when the G-8 under Mr. Blair's (Prime Minister of Britain) presidency took Ethiopia in the fold. Blair's effort to write this human success story was frustrated when the Ethiopians failed to take the opportunity by bungling their June 2005 elections.

Perhaps as another manifestation of increased control and stranglehold of G^4 management is the greater freedom the elite of society are beginning to have in Ethiopia. Educated Ethiopians are turning down government job offers signaling ethnic or religious affiliations.[48] This is in spite of demonstrated destructive opportunism in EPRDF's use of ethnic and religious differences in the country.

The management of G^4 cannot be complacent about its complete control or mastery of the Ethiopian and Horn of Africa situation. The management of G^4 may exhaust all its resources in Iraq, Afghanistan and Pakistan if it failed to win the war there quickly. If China and Russia misinterpreted the honest signals sent to them by the G^4 management, they could throw the whole of humanity back to the cold war era, although in the process it is they who are likely to lose the most. The Americans may decide to withdraw believing that they paid too much for nothing, leaving the Afghans to fend for themselves, and forgetting their involvement in causing the disaster in the first place. On the other hand, through the acceptance of the principle of conversion into G^4, both China and Russia would be able to cooperate with the G^4 management, place themselves on a sustainable course of private property development and lead in solving the problems of humanity (in Iraq, Pakistan, Afghanistan, the environmental crises, the world economic crises of the century, etc.) including establishment of good-governance government in Ethiopia or the Horn of Africa region.

Even if China and Russia cooperated with the G^4 management on the Ethiopian case, the Ethiopian conversion into good-governance government has its own problems. The fruitless "befriend all" policy being pursued by the G^4 management is making the EPRDF and the political opposition parties unwieldy and uncompromising, and they need to be told of their irrelevance to the shaping of Ethiopia's future, which is now firmly in the hands of the G^4 management.[49]

---

[48] Ethiopians on the whole have the same sensitivities and objections to any discrimination outside affirmative action programmes as Americans, especially discriminations based on race, religion or gender.

[49] After all it is the G^4 management that negotiated with the Soviets to leave the region and for the Derg to disband when these were forces outside its control. One would

It is to be recalled that toward the end of the Derg rule, Addis Ababa was rescued by the G^4 management from eminent catastrophe. G^4 Management was able to work with the Derg and through an emergency operation the utility services of the Town were restored. Since then the Town's administration was destroyed and professionals who tried to provide service under very difficult circumstances left or were dismissed by the EPRDF administration. Today, when the G^4 management has complete control Addis Abebans are waiting for accidents to happen: Demand for utility services has skyrocketed and the town population has increased while supply is practically where the last G^4 rescue mission left it. The city administration is in disarray and lacks professional competence to maintain basic services and cannot carry out planning.

Alleged Somali terrorists and former employees of the Siad Barre government in Somalia, tribal party leaders and covert religious movement leaders were given leadership positions in the EPRDF Government. These having captured the government media were spewing hatred, descent, misinformation and xenophobia. It all happened at a time when G^4 management has taken full control of developments in Ethiopia, and these destructions have been fully or partially financed by G^4 itself.

The waiting game harms everybody. There is also the intergenerational problem emanating from this game which if allowed to complete its course is likely to bring irrecoverable damage to economy and society. Waiting means waiting for the destructors to pass away, but it also means to let the solution to the problem (e.g. the elites of society) to pass away as well. Waiting means for the children of Pr5 and their associates in government as well as the children of the occupiers of the XHS housing project to rule and to confront the formidable and angry force of the children of the oppressed, of the children of the elites denied their rights to serve society and of millions whose human and property rights have been violated and all those others whose grievances the G^4 management has failed to address on time. The Derg used 12 or 13 of its 17 years of rule in the destruction of lives (mainly the lives of the elites of society) and private property. Waiting means missing this opportunity to start on a

expect it must be relatively easy now to make any arrangement that the G^4 management wishes when all are breathing the air it gives them.

clean plate. Compare that to Russia and the difficulties being faced by the Russian government to convert the huge collectivist property to private property or public property.

The effect of G^4's indecisiveness is to increase transaction costs for the management of G^4 and to make its control slip through the fingers. G^4 cannot address the Ethiopian people through alleged wrongdoers and criminals whether they are in government or outside government. G^4 cannot bring about harmony and reconciliation by a meeting with the allegedly guilty party. The reconciliation is not between them but between those that wronged or allegedly wronged society and the society at large.

Therefore, the G^4 management has to move quickly on many fronts if it is to succeed in this case where it has worked and succeeded to have a fully controlled situation. The EPRDF and some of the opposition parties who were its former allies have charges placed against them by international human right organizations, EHRO and eyewitness accounts of criminal deeds which have not been investigated so far. The G^4 management seems to have paved the way for these groups and individuals to be able to face those charges. This process must get closure by negotiating and providing an exit plan for those who are innocent of the alleged charges of crimes.

The solution to the problem faced by the people of Ethiopia (which is establishment of good-governance government in that country) is intertwined with the problems faced by the larger society of the Africa Horn area and can be provided by G^4 management working in collaboration with the people and the elite of society. All the elite of society today live under the protection of G^4 management. It is these elite who treasure the social assets of the larger society, that are proud of the *Geez* cultural heritage[50], that see value in the role played by various religion and ethnic groups in cementing and bringing out the sense of

---

[50] That is what Getachew Haile is doing through his translation and explanations of ancient works of Geez. Daniel Admassie built a lasting monument to the memory of the artist who crafted artistic letters of the Geez by mounting the *Yigezu font* on the word processor. Many historians, artists, economists and anthropologists, scientists and other professionals (including those from the area) have been and are making important contributions to create awareness and solidarity in the region.

oneness in the larger society. It is the elite of the larger society that recognize their common heritage and destiny. G^4 can facilitate dialogue among the elite of society and create an enabling environment for their effective participation in the political and economic transformation of society and economy.

In the framework of the principal-agent theory, the principal must pay some attention to the case and must review the role of the agent[51] and provide guidance so that the management of G^4 will be able to succeed in the least difficult and least costly of the many difficult and costly problems it is confronted with in the world today. Therefore, G^4 management must immediately start a dialogue with the Ethiopian people and the people of the Horn whose life and destiny are intertwined and ensure the elite of society should be given the liberty to play a role in the reconstruction and development of economy and society.

---

[51] In this case the agent may act opportunistically to benefit from the prolongation of the situation in situ, i.e. maintaining the status quo. It is also observed that the agent is mismanaging the transformation programme by increased frequency of turnover of agency personnel and by not using people who have an understanding of the history, politics and economics of the place.

4. The "Revelation of the Good-Governance Government

The fundamental problem of economics is about resource scarcity and competition over scarce resources. One approach toward the solution of this problem would be to "do what the animals around humans do", which is to wait for nature to provide and when there isn't enough to go around to be governed by the rule of the animal world: the survival of the fittest.

But, humans believe they have the cognitive capacity and the will to change things. Going through the philosophical discourse of individualism, utilitarianism and rationalism, the economist arrives at some conclusions regarding the nature and motivations of man. Accordingly, man is assumed rational, i.e. man has faculties to store, process and analyze data in a logical and consistent way and can arrive at an independent decision. This natural trait is reflected in man's creative ability, i.e. man's ability to discover and invent new products and new ways of doing things.

Regarding motivation, the assumption is made that man is driven by hedonistic utilitarianism which postulates that utility, the "greatest happiness principle", provides the philosophical bases or guidance in ethical behavior and decision making. This desire for "happiness", it is assumed, is driven by production and consumption of goods and services, i.e. private property development.[52]

The development of private property forms both the *cause* and the *object* or consequence of human creativity, in the sense that in order to be creative or make optimal use of human creativity man needs a conducive environment and a part of this environment is freedom of thought and action plus material amenities which make application possible. Man needs the laboratories, internet access, food, education, health service, entertainment, secure and comfortable living, i.e. private property

---

[52] Altruism and non-material or non-economic things can also be sources of human "happiness". But these are interconnected with human creativity and the production of goods and services, i.e. private property development. All humans have kindness and generosity in them and are desirous of fulfilling the Ten Commandments of the Bible (drawing satisfaction or happiness from doing so). But it is the one who has goods and services to offer that gives meaning to the kindness and generosity in man. It makes little sense to talk about "not to steal" or "not to kill" without the existence of something to steal and a reason for killing.

development. The purpose of exploiting creative ability also becomes production and consumption of new goods and services and new ways of doing things, i.e. private property development.

Thus, based on this philosophical foundation, the economist assumes the firm aims at profit maximization and by so doing produces the maximum amounts and diversities of best quality goods and services at minimum cost. And, the consumer maximizes her/his utility from the consumption of those goods and services produced given incomes and market prices.

This translation into the goal of *private property development* is something over which the economist cannot compromise. Within the purview of rationalism, (not going into religion, or belief systems generally and occult practices), this appears to be the logical premise on which economic theories are founded.

When we emphasize individualism in private property development, it does not mean that the individual exercises or does his/her creative work and discovery always in isolation. This days lone discoveries like the theory of gravity by watching apples fall on the head seem to be rare occurrences. Today human creativity is best realized in team work. In addition to the acquisition of cognitive skills through formal education the facilities for human creativity and applications such as the laboratories, websites and access to the websites, and the business organizations are required and they form a part of the private property system. Some of the private business organizations such as the multinationals have greater paying capacity, better incentives and provide a more conducive working environment for human creativity and hence for the development of private property than government.

Economic historians assume private property development evolved from common property. Among the pre-right property systems the most well known is *common property*, that is property that is owned by a community of people as a group. In property evolutionary theory, this property system transits or ends up into any one of the following property systems: (a) becomes the "the tragedy of the commons" like pastoralist areas of Ethiopia and agricultural lands in the North of the country becoming wastelands or a part of the desert as a result of desert encroachment or overuse and abuse of the land and water resources, (b) gets converted into private property, (c) public property, or (d) collectivist property.

Collectivist property belongs to government and its purpose is *to replace* private property. In the USSR private employment of the means of production was forbidden by law and the communist state permitted only one type of property to exist there - Collectivist property. Over 80 percent of the USSR GDP was produced in a collectivist property - government owned enterprises, cooperatives and state farms. The collectivist property can also be regarded as a pre-right property system, since it had no legislation and protection for private property rights. It was to establish the system of collectivist property development that the Derg undertook its program of destruction of private property and society.

What obtains in Communist China is quite different. The communist government concluded agreements with private companies (foreign direct investment), allowed their establishment in China and agreed to legislation and protection of *private property rights*.

4.1 Property, Property Rights, and the Law

If you looked into the magic box labeled *private property* (Box A in Figure 2) today in a modern economy, such as the USA, the things that you see include: pencils, paper, mobile, land, buildings, kettle, bread, house, shirts, vehicles, handguns, camera etc.[53] You also get wide ranging

---

[53] *Private property* is classified into two: real property and personal property. *Real property* (also called immovable property) refers to land, land improvement, buildings, machinery and equipment tied to land. *Personal property* is movable property or non-real property and, in turn, is classified into *tangible personal property* (or corporeal property) and *intangible* (incorporeal) *personal property*. Examples of corporeal or tangible personal properties are cars, tables, mobile, personal effects, etc. Incorporeal or intangible personal properties include negotiable (financial) instruments of the money and capital markets. They also include *pure intangibles* such as property rights to a contract or bond, patent, trademark and copyright. A variety of non-marketable securities also form a part of the intangible personal property system. Examples include rights to inheritance or gift and nonnegotiable securities such as government bonds (kept by holder until maturity) and most certificates of bank deposits (such as CDs). The category of *intangible social assets* or social capital includes non-compete

services including haircuts, music show, dental repairs, cinema, opera, football game, garage services, etc. In the evolution of private property development most recent introductions to the stock of private properties include *intangible assets* (e.g. financial instruments of the money and capital markets); *quantifiable intangible assets*, or contractual rights to use another's property or non-compete agreements (such as monopoly rights, franchise rights, leasehold rights and licenses). There are also *unquantifiable intangible assets* (e.g. goodwill, customer satisfaction, corporate culture and strategy, union solidarity, law abidingness); and *intellectual property rights* (e.g. patents, copyrights, and trade marks) as a part of the private property system. Finally, the system of private property rights also includes *social assets* (a generic term for things like good governance, progressive social values, common decency, group solidarity and cooperation, etc.) which affect individual behavior and decision making.

Figure 1: Types of Private Property of a Mature Market Economy

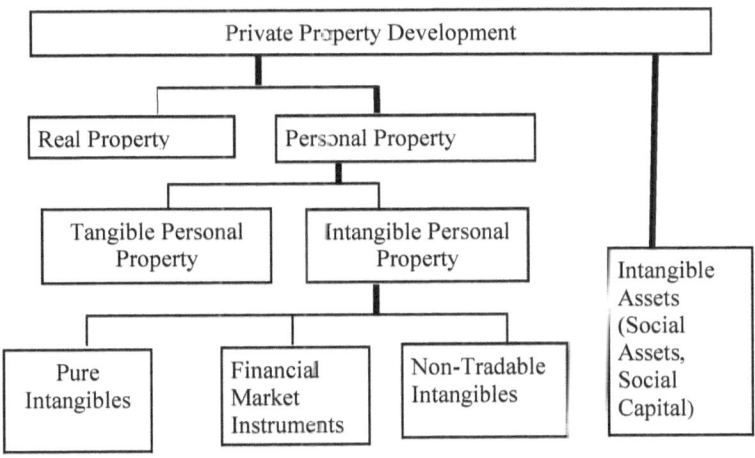

Private property is different from *private property rights*. Property rights relate to the legal entitlements, i.e. the legislation and protection given to the proprietor. For the effective development of private property we need

---

agreements or contracts such as monopoly rights, franchise rights, leasehold rights and licenses. These are called *quantifiable intangible assets*. There are also *unquantifiable intangible assets* such as goodwill, customer satisfaction, corporate culture and strategy, cooperation, employee loyalty, and law abidingness which impact on private property development and hence business success.

laws and we also need the institutions or bureaucracy for the implementation of the laws.[54] Properties existed in ancient times, but property rights did not exist in those times. To understand the concept of property rights and property claims we go back to 1970 and see what government was trying to do by way of introducing law and order in property development in Ethiopia. Feudal landlords in Addis Ababa had uncontested land claims, but to convert these into property rights or claim rights, it was necessary to legislate (passage by parliament of property law), establish the AA Municipality with legal mandate to issue title-deeds and establish also the courts, police, i.e. the bureaucracy to ensure that the law is implemented correctly and justly. The bureaucracy normally provides public service (like fire brigade putting out fire, the courts adjudicating, and the investment office licensing), and keeps public records (archival service). Had the Derg not destroyed the 30 years of effort at reform, the next generation of Addis Abebans would have exchanged these title-deeds or rights to property in the property market, just as one exchanges or takes possession of a box of matches upon payment of price.

Private property rights and public property rights are legal notions. The rights refer to the legislation and protection of those properties. If you take your house as an example of private property, the rights pertain to your possession of a title-deed to land and a certificate of ownership to the house. This ownership right defines your legal entitlements as owner of the house. Thus, you can paint the house, rent the house, mortgage the house, get a plumber to fix the leaking pipes in the house, and hang your picture on the wall of the house. There are many "correlated" rights to your ownership of the house, with each such right implying relationships with different persons or organizations and associated rights and duties. For example, when you rented the house you have a right to the collection

---

[54] Although property laws show variations among jurisdictions (national legal systems and notions of international law have evolved from diverse roots, e.g. the Sharia), there are basically two articulated systems which can serve as models for the developing countries: *common law* and *civil law* jurisdictions. Roughly, common law systems originate in customary unwritten laws and today when laws are written the courts often base their verdict on customary practice and precedent cases; while there is greater reliance on codification of laws and referencing to specific provisions in the law in the case of civil law adjudication.

of rent and the tenant has a user right to the house and a duty to pay the rent. Your engaging of the plumber is likely to operate on the basis of contract (written or unwritten) which entitles you to the service and puts a duty on you to pay the plumber. The law spells out these rights and duties, and it is these relationships between people in relation to the property, in this case the house, which we refer to as private property rights.[55]

Many people see the right of ownership as establishing a legal relationship between the owner and the property he/she owns, in this case the house. But this is wrong; there cannot be a legal "relationship" between an inanimate object, the house, and a human being. *Property right is a legal relationship between people in relation to the property*, in this case the house. There may be legal restrictions to the house proprietorship, for example, you cannot broadcast loud music from the house and there are the municipality ordinances which may put certain limitations on your ownership or user rights to the house.

As a corollary of the above, the correlated rights of a house vary across time and space. Thus, ownership rights to the house and the correlated rights to the ownership of the house today will be different from the package of associated rights next year. Likewise, the ownership and correlated rights of two houses in the same neighborhood may vary; for example, owner of house A may rent a room, owner of house B may not rent rooms but may carry out renovation work. Ownership portfolio in two different towns may spell out different packages of rights and correlated rights reflecting the different city ordinances in use.

Box 8: Differences in the Conception of "Ownership Rights" to Property

> The time was 1980 and the place Geneva, Switzerland. Three
> economists (an Ethiopian from Addis Ababa, a Soviet citizen from

---

[55] How about your father's house in a remote village in Arsi? Your father may have an uncontested ownership claim over the house, but there are no ordinances and bureaucracies for the certification of ownership and the protection of the property rights of your father. There is hardly any dispute arising from your father's claim of ownership of the house in the village. In a modern society however, the peace and tranquillity of the village is not there and one needs the title-deeds, city ordinances, and bureaucracies in order to have an orderly existence in a modern city.

Moscow and a US American) held a discussion on "personal ownership of apartments". All three use "ownership" in the way they understand it, but obviously for the onlooker they mean different things. When the soviet person talks about her "ownership" of an apartment, she means she has government "permission" (subject to written and unwritten rules, but where the unwritten rules often matter more) to live in the apartment which belongs to government, and may even believe that governments own apartments everywhere in the world. When the American speaks of his "ownership" of the apartment, myriads of "rights" cross his mind: the right of ownership (title deed), the right to live in (consume), mortgage, transfer (as a gift or inheritance), sell, rent, or exchange. There are also correlated rights relating to financing of the apartment, contracts with civil engineers, brokerage firms and individuals, banks, decorators and renovators, gardeners, utility providers, etc. - all related to his ownership of the apartment and involving legal contracts in which rights and duties are spelt out. What also cross the mind of the American is the legalism (legislation, bureaucracy, mechanisms and procedures) surrounding "ownership" and all the "correlated" rights. The American cannot hold a prolonged discussion with the other two without seeking clarification or specification of the property rights they are talking about. The Ethiopian may explain what "ownership" meant to him in 1970, but in 1980 he may not be sure of what to say. In 1970 the Ethiopian's understanding of "ownership" may come close to that of the American, because property legislation (for example, the Commercial Code, the Civil Code, and the ordinances of the Municipality of Addis Ababa) was patterned on American and Western practice. The Ethiopian may even quote some government directive (e.g. the directive of the Derg which sets a ceiling for floor area of the house of $180\,m^2$, which according to rumors was later reduced to $70\,m^2$) or explain his "understanding" that no individual could own an apartment in 1980 Ethiopia.

In the year 2009 when these three individuals meet again to discuss the concept of "ownership", the American is once again clear on what is meant by private "ownership" of an apartment. To be sure there has been more legislation, expansion of the bureaucracy, increased varieties of private property rights and derivative rights in the USA - all added-up on what was there in 1980. But the Russian is no longer sure she understands the concept of "ownership", "private property rights", etc. in 2009. The Ethiopian, who was emulating the Soviet person or living under a government patterned on the Soviets in 1980, must now be directionless once again and unable to participate in a discussion on private property ownership.

> The American conception and practice of private property development is anchored on the notion of good-governance government and is a result of centuries of evolutionary struggles in social problem solving. One must therefore start with the concept of property rights in order to understand how private property rights should be organized.

It is to be concluded, therefore, that the law and public bureaucracy are necessary for the sustainable development of private property. In a modern market economy there are basically two types of properties: public property and private property. *Public property* is property which belongs to government; and its purpose is to enhance and to complement private property development.[56] Using heuristic and syllogistic methods of reasoning it can be concluded there is no other purpose for public property development. In certain cases markets (for private goods) may be *non-existent*, and supplying these goods and services by government becomes the justification for public property development. That is, there are certain goods and services which are necessary for social consumption which the market cannot supply; e.g. nuclear energy in Egypt, a railway service in Ethiopia connecting Addis Ababa to the ports, or water supply to the Town. When it is possible for private companies to supply nuclear energy in Egypt, rail service and water in Ethiopia, government is expected to privatize the public companies because market provision of these goods is more efficient. There are a large number of goods called pure public goods[57] and services which are provided by government for this reason, e.g. national defense, waterways, highways, street lighting, etc.

There are also cases where *market fails*, e.g. externalities, decreasing cost industries, etc., to provide goods and services or where private suppliers can provide them but at high price. Here again, government intervention can take many forms, e.g. government can use regulation, subsidize private producers, create partnerships with private suppliers, or produce them in public enterprises.

---

[56] Compare this to collectivist property which is *to replace* private property.

[57] Pure public goods are non-excludable and non-rival in consumption. Mixed public goods include club goods (which are excludable and non-rival) and common pool resources (which are nonexcludable and rivalrous in consumption)

In some other cases market efficiency calls for government provision of *public policy*. Public policy often takes the form of legislation and covers a much wider ground, for example, may relate to solving social problems (e.g. curving drug addiction, child abuse, crime, rape, etc.), and political problems (e.g. human right protection, citizenship law, protection of minorities, and devolution of power). Public policies applied to economic or property issues take many forms. Highly skewed income distribution can cause social disturbance and government can contain the situation by using fiscal policy, e.g. progressive income taxation. Likewise inflation, which can affect the rate of return on investment, can be contained by a combination of fiscal policy, e.g. increase of income tax rate, reduction of public expenditures, etc. and monetary policy, e.g. decreasing money supply, increasing interest rate, etc.

Thus, the kinds of things we observe in the box labeled "*public policy and public property development*" (Box B in the Figure) include public goods, public service, public enterprises, bureaucracies and policies or government legislation. Regarding the law, reference could be made to specific legislation pertaining to private property development, e.g. contract law, property law, trust law, copyright law, etc. In the Ethiopian case, the Civil Code and the Commercial Code of Ethiopia provide specific legislation on property.[58] Public enterprises relate to economic organizations owned by government such as the Ethiopian Telecommunication Authority, power generating dams, highways, and public utilities, government pharmaceutical and manufacturing plants. When these investments crowed out private investments they fail to represent the true functions of public property, which is to complement and enhance private property development.

Public policy in the form of government legislation may not necessarily be guided by the principle of complementing or enhancing private property development. For example, the "Cattle Tax" legislation of the 1950s was a failure in that it lacked fiscal administration and the pastoralists were not money using. During the early days of the Derg rule, any pronouncement by any of the hundred some members of the junta were considered government "decrees", forcefully implemented by the armed cadres of the

---

[58] Although it is difficult to tell today which law is repealed, discarded or upheld.

system. These "decrees" lacked legitimacy, consistent application, and were introduced to violate (not protect) human and property rights. We also see in today's Ethiopia regional administration rulers and bureaucracy heads making such tax "legislations" and procedural rulings without proper constitutional or legal mandates, and resulting in violations of private property and human rights.

Sometimes the relationship between private and public property development may not be clear. Take, for example, the statue at the market place. If it were in Moscow in 1970 it would be identified as collective property, in New York City it is public property and in Ethiopia it depends on the time and its function and on how you view government. For a statue to qualify as *public property* there must be a good-governance government ruling behind it. Does it contribute to private property development? The answer will be yes in the case of public property, albeit indirectly. The statue instills in the minds of the onlooker values such as bravery in battle, benevolence, beneficence, altruism, innovation, discovery, public service, etc. all essential qualities in man and determinants of private property development. By going through the mill (good-governance government), it becomes the property of all citizens and they are willing (voluntarily) to defend and protect it. For individual commemoration, the statues are often erected posthumously in order to avoid the risk of revision of public decisions. Compare this to African dictators who erect their statue (is it collectivist property, private property or public property?) while in office and witness its destruction by the mob in their own lifetime. What they erected in the name of the people becomes in this case a "personal property" claim, not a claim right. It is not a private property, in the sense used here because legally sanctioned personal properties emanate from property and human right legislation and protection. It is not public property either, because apart from fulfilling the legal and procedural requirement to qualify as public property, the statue also fails to convey the public purpose which is to enhance and complement private property development.[59]

---

[59] One need not undervalue the importance of public property development. The aim here is to underscore the point that public policy and public property development is undertaken in order to enhance and complement private property development.

In the same way it is difficult to classify Radio Fana, ETV, the government press, Endowment Fund for the Rehabilitation of Tigray (EFFORT), etc. as public properties for two reasons: (a) the legal basis for all or for some of them (and whether or not they emanate from decisions of a good-governance government) is uncertain, and (b) the purpose is not necessarily to enhance or complement private property development. Regarding (b) the aim may be to crowed out private investment in those activities, for example. One can argue that the Ethiopian Telecommunication Authority (ETA) could be a public property at its establishment, but today when the private market can offer telecommunication services more efficiently it only serves to crowed out private investment in the telecommunications industry, i.e. does not enhance or complement private property development. Therefore, the ETA loses its public property status today.[60]

It is not only the law and the bureaucracy, public policy and public property that are needed in order to create the conducive environment for private property development. Government, even a good-governance government is limited in what it can offer for optimal tapping of individual creativity and resourcefulness. That is why society needs the free press, the civil society organizations, the human rights and women rights advocacy groups, the NGOs, professional associations, cultural groups and the moral societies (like religions, belief systems, etc.)[61]. Government needs these, (a) to take off the cost load on the budget, and (b) they also complement and enhance private property development and therefore share with government the task of carrying out this task. Society needs the operators in Box C to provide the public a wide range of goods and services and choices which the private market (Box A) and government (Box B) do not offer. Under good-governance government, government encourages what you observe inside the box labeled Box C in Figure 2. The activities of those institutions and organizations in Box C are supported by government with collaborative work, licensing, enhancing and enabling legislation and funding.

---

[60] For public policy or public enterprise, debate and passage of the establishment legislation by (the parliament of) a good-governance government is a necessary requirement. In the Ethiopian case public property development may even be more required because of lacking private property development.

[61] Note all these belong to private legal entities, i.e. Box A.

Putting the three parts together, we have the system for sustainable private property development in a modern market economy depicted below.

Figure 2: The System of Private Property Development

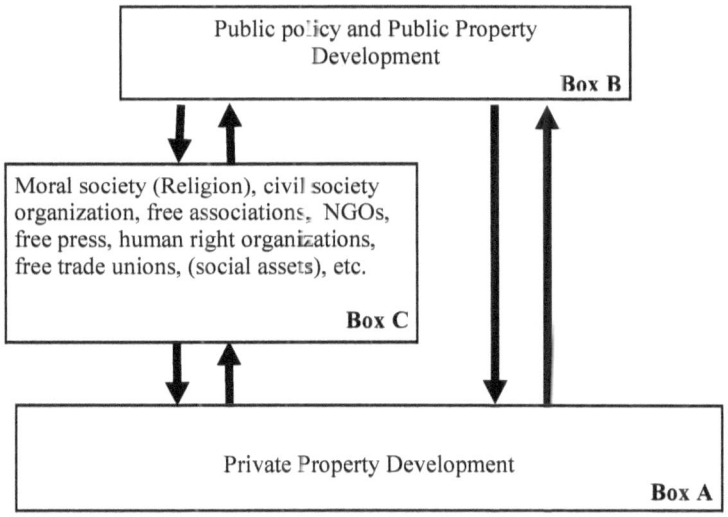

The arrow from Box A to Box B represents flow of resources such as tax revenue, charges, fees for government service, individual social security contributions, financial and other resources or properties left in banks without will or for government collections, and returns from government investments. The greater the volume of resource flow the stronger government becomes in its capacity to deal with delivery of government service.

The arrow from Box B to Box A represents the flow of public goods, public enterprise outputs, public policy (legislation), public service (bureaucratic service), public information, and upkeep of public records. The bureaucrat may be driven by self interest but not necessarily driven by destructively opportunistic behavior. Among the things government can do in order to encourage departure from destructive opportunistic behavior is to create conditions favorable for such things as honor, prestige, public service, basic human decency to play roles in influencing the bureaucrat's (or the agent's) behavior, in addition to establishing moral codes and improving the incentive systems. This can be done with the help of forces in Box C, e.g. the moral society and the free media.

The arrow from Box B to Box C includes flows of legislation or government policy (encouraging the establishment of Box C actors, by giving licenses, facilitating registration and operation rules, etc.), funding, and cooperation in their common endeavors to enhance and complement private property development. The flow from C to B includes tax revenues, funding, cooperation and guidance.

Regarding the flow of resources from Box A to Box C, suppose a businessperson wanted to establish a foundation to support blind students. To enable the businessperson achieve his desires, society must first ensure that a government department, authority, institution or organization is established by law to handle such foundation "businesses". Then the businessperson can establish his foundation on the basis of rules and procedures established by that government authority and operate freely in the system. Among the concerns of the public and government is the source of fund for the foundation. Society and the government authority must establish that "good" money is always used to establish foundations, i.e. ensure that stolen money, drug money or any money acquired illegally is not used.

For a sustainable private property development (see framework or the Figure above), there obtains a strict definition of the relationship between the three blocks – Private property development (Box A), Public policy and public property development(Box B), and the middle block (Box C). The expected relationship between them is a *mutualistic symbiotic relationship* and not a *parasitical* or *commensal symbiotic relationship*.

Unless society viewed the whole system of private property development, with its three-way partitioning for analytical convenience as an organic whole, there is very little that can be achieved by tempering with parts of it. When we talk of reform in this case, it is a reform that takes into cognizance the interconnectedness of the whole system of private property development. Put that way, the framework depicted in the diagram represents the essence of good governance. Good-governance government relates to the structure of the polity for optimum production and consumption of private property.

4.2 Good Governance[62] and Good-Governance Government

The United Nations Millennium Summit of 2000 adopted the *UN Millennium Declaration*, which, inter alia, identifies "human rights, democracy and good governance" as its priority policy objectives for the 21st century. Many international organizations including the United Nations Development Program (UNDP), UN Office of the High Commission for Human Rights (UN-OHCHR), the World Bank, the International Monetary Fund (IMF), world centers on governance research and OECD have been working on the theme of "good governance". The outcome of this concerted effort includes World-wide consensus formation on a common definition, commitment to establish systems of good governance everywhere, and application of good governance criteria in providing aid to the least developed countries. Good governance as presently conceived is applicable for all member states of the United Nations, not just the developing and least-developed country groupings. The Least developed countries (numbering 49 of which 34 are African) are especially vulnerable to the good-governance requirement for grants and development loans because they lack the domestic means of finance to extricate themselves from the vicious circle of poverty and underdevelopment, and some of them, to cover recurrent expenditures of government. Good governance is not a static concept but a dynamic one, evolving all the time to remove constraints on human-rights and liberty-rights and addressing the governance issues of the times. As it now stands, good governance contains the following elements.

---

[62] Legislation and bureaucratization were indicated in the forgoing discussions as the necessary conditions for "sustainable private property development". The sufficient conditions are provided by probing deep into the nature of government, including "good governance".

4.2.1 Good Governance Means Democratic Governance

Democracy is a system of governance in which the people exercise power and control of government through voluntary participation. The government is a representation of the will of the people and is charged by them with the task of protecting human rights, liberty rights, claim rights and minority rights. In democracies periodic elections take place in which the people voluntarily make their choices in the selection of political parties to rule and approve government priority programs. Other features of a democracy include its foundation in constitutionalism; legality and rule of law; the separation of powers (as between the legislature and the executive branches of government); independent judiciary; existence, independence and participation in governance of political parties (multipartism), free media, civil societies, professional groups, etc.; and peaceful coexistence of different religions, cultures, social groups, tribes, and political views.

In a democracy the citizen participates in government directly, for example in a plebiscite, and indirectly through elected representatives. Majority rule, as this practice is called, is an expression of good governance, and assumes responsible behavior on the part of government as well as the electorate,[63] which, among other things, is also entrusted with the duty to comply with government regulation.

Constitutionalism is the principle that the authority of government derives from the law and is limited by law or constitution; and rule of law implies that officers of government, including presidents and prime ministers, and the bureaucracy perform their constitutional duties according to the law.[64] The principle of constitutionalism also implies that the constitution is accepted by all the people, who make a commitment to honor and protect

---

[63] In many countries, holding of private property rights and educational qualifications had been obligatory requirements for partaking in a democratic process. In other cases additional requirements (e.g. race and gender) were added to establish "responsible behavior" in the conduct of democracy.

[64] This need not suggest legalism, which refers to the principle of strict adherence to the letter, rather than the spirit, of the law.

it.[65] In a democracy, nobody is above the law, and citizens and officers of government are bound together by their common trust in each other, desire to the exercise of right, and a commitment to duty and respect for the constitution and rule of law.

Nevertheless, gross violations of the principles of majority rule have been commonplace throughout history and in many parts of the globe. Theocracies, ethnocracies, dictatorships and a variety of xenophobic groups are known to impose their will on the minority, e.g. the German Nazis, the Hutu majority in Rwanda, the Muslims in Iraq against the Christian minority, the government of Georgia in Southern Ossetia and Abkhazia, the liberation movements of "peoples, nations and nationalities" in the Horn area, etc. There are also cases where a minority government imposes its will on the majority, e.g. the whites in Southern Rhodesia, and in South Africa during the Apartheid period, the Tutsi dominated government in Rwanda, Tigray Peoples' Liberation Front (TPLF) or the Government of the Ethiopian Peoples Revolutionary Democratic Front (EPRDF) in Ethiopia, etc.

Other violations of democratic precepts of governance are also commonplace in today's world. Dictators declare their claims to rule for life emanate from a demonstrated expression of the wishes of the people; they promulgate tirelessly, create new bureaucracies and proliferate red-tapes endlessly; use the government, bureaucracy and parliament to rubberstamp their decisions and serve their sectarian interests (i.e. the interests of the dictator, ethnocracy, theocracy or ruling party); hold mass rallies and conduct bogus elections in which close to 100 percent of the electorate participate and elect them into office; and all these in vain, hoping that somehow they would be able to succeed in coercing the people (especially the opposition groups) into submission, and dupe the international community into believing that they are democratic and practicing "good governance".

Good governance means only elected officers of government and/or legally appointed individuals into public office are entrusted with the

---

[65] This is not to suggest inflexibility or non-changeability in the constitution. Indeed, the constitution should be viewed as a document to be consolidated by specific legislations and capable of accommodating revisions and amendments to become inclusive and adjusting to changing circumstance.

duties and functions of government. However, in a number of African countries "kitchen Cabinets" (informal advisors involving non-elected officials in public office) run governments, while elected officials play subsidiary roles, are dismissed from office or even incarcerated or killed, in contravention of the constitution and rule of law. Civilian control and authority over the military and police, which are fundamental to democracy and good governance, are not necessarily practiced in many African countries. Instead, the police and military are hijacked by organized groups and serve sectional interests. In a number of cases government lacks legitimacy and instead of serving the whole nation and being accountable to the whole population, it serves the interests of a particular group and is not accountable to the people. It is also common practice for powerful and influential groups (including criminal groups) to exert considerable influence on government through economic, family, ethnic, religious or ideological connections.

An important post-2000 development has been the decision by the European Union, the government of the U.S.A., World Bank and the IMF, the UNDP and other aid donors to poor countries to implement the "human rights, democracy and good governance" provisions of the UN-Millennium Declaration in matters of aid and as a guiding principle in any and all intergovernmental relations.[66] International aid or grant to poor countries is today divided into two: *humanitarian aid* (or food-aid) is looked at as human-right or liberty-right, and there is commitment on the part of the international community to provide it to all those in need; while *development aid* is given to those governments that meet the conditions of good governance.

While governments of resource rich dictatorships, theocracies, and ethnocracies may delay reform to establish "good governance" at their peril,[67] the governments of the least developed countries cannot afford to overlook the need for immediate reform, since they have no independent domestic means and are heavily dependent on foreign aid and loans both

---

[66] It does not necessarily mean that there is a universal agreement over the definition of "human rights, democracy and good governance", or imply that this provision is not used as a cover to channel aid to embolden dictators in Africa and elsewhere.

[67] Not to reform, among other things, will constrain their participation in the globalization process.

to finance food security and development; and in some cases to finance recurrent budget expenditures of government. Today, some of the governments of these poor countries, e.g. Somalia, Eritrea, Ethiopia, and Rwanda subsist by "budget support" from donor communities and their "partners in development".

4.2.2 Freedoms, Liberties and Responsible behavior

Good governance cannot be practiced in and by a society of slaves, or where there are individuals or groups whose human rights, claim-rights and liberty-rights are curtailed. Good governance implies fostering freedoms and guaranteeing and protecting the human-rights and liberty-rights of the individual.

The citizen exercises her/his rights in a variety of ways, for example, through free speech, demonstration, and voting for change. Good governance also means responsible behavior, which is expressed by the individual's participation in mandatory military service (in some democracies), serving in a jury (a practice in the U.S.A. justice system), paying taxes, implementing other duties assigned by law or government, and respecting the rights of others. Responsible behavior on the side of officials of government and the bureaucracy means that they perform their duties on the basis of the law and are guided in their actions by the principles of constitutionalism, legalism and rule of law.

The individual as well as officers of government can enjoy their claim-rights and liberty-rights and perform their duties in a responsible way if they are knowledgeable about the constitution and the law and accountable for their actions. That is why good governance depends upon a free, literate and knowledgeable citizenry, and its effective participation in all aspects of the democratic process.

4.2.3 Participation and Inclusiveness

Inclusiveness and participation are the hallmarks of good governance. "Inclusiveness" refers to the inclusion of men and women, political parties, civil societies, and other stakeholders in government.

"Participation" implies partaking freely and peacefully in development, conflict resolution, decision making, elections and other democratic governance processes. It also means that the citizen, as an individual or in a group formation, participates in the formulation of ideas, development of long-run perspective plans, policies and programs, program implementation, monitoring and follow-up. A more common participation of the citizen in government is through membership into Political parties, civil society organizations, professional societies, trade unions, employers' associations, chambers of commerce, free media society, philanthropic organizations, consumer society organizations, lobby groups, human right organizations, etc.

Political parties interconnect the individual or the people and the government. They recruit, campaign, mobilize people around a cause, get elected into office, and offer society political choice. It is widely expected that political parties in a democracy practice the principles of tolerance, compromise and governing by coalitions. Good governance as a political goal is attained when political parties air their differences in a transparent manner and succeed to work together as a team for the common good of society.

Like political parties, many civil society organizations or non-governmental organizations empower the citizen and enrich the life of the larger society. They give the individual choice and a chance to participate in good governance through mobilizing individuals with different backgrounds to come and work together, build and learn new skills, develop relationships, trust each other, and share common values.

In some African fledgling democracies there is a tendency to use the constitution and the law or authority of public office to curb claim rights and liberty rights of citizens and to criminalize opposition parties.[68] There are also frequent disagreements between some African governments and international non-governmental organizations such as Amnesty International, Human Rights Watch, International Association of Journalists and humanitarian organizations. The international NGOs

---

[68] Examples include the Kenyan and Zimbabwe elections of 2008, and the Ethiopian election of 2005.

accuse government for violating the rights of its citizens and of meddling in their affairs, while the government accuses the NGOs for illegal interference in the affairs of government and otherwise overstepping the limits of their work agreements with them.

Multi-pronged approaches are being taken in order to improve the state of democratic governance in Africa and globally. It has been indicated that at the level of the United Nations and multilateral credit banks there is a growing commitment to apply the good governance criteria both in the management of aid and in all matters of intergovernmental relations. American Panel on the Nonprofit Sector (2007) have recently issued a guide for charities and foundations, which brings the work they do in Africa and elsewhere into harmony with the 2000 UN Millennium Declaration.[69]

4.2.4 Transparency and Accountability

The production and management of information is an expensive business, and one that is indispensable for the practice of good governance. Government is best placed both to produce and manage information optimally.

In the private economy, information asymmetry[70] often leads to constricted competition, lack of transparency, increase in transaction costs and market failure. In the public sector, information asymmetry gives rise to the tragedy of the commons and the free rider problem in the provision of public goods, moral hazard in risk-averse strategies open for holders of public office[71], and in general, to "the principal-agent problem" or "agency dilemma" arising from the conflicting interest between the citizen or electorate (principal) and holder of public office (the agent) (Stiglitz,

---

[69] It is to be noted that a criticism of NGO aid to poor countries has been that that the NGOs are using the aid as a cover to export dissent and conflict in society and place a wedge between the people and the government. The NGOs are now saying we do not carry out activities which are not approved by our government and are not inline with the Millennium Declaration.

[70] Where relevant information is not equally accessible to all participants in a transaction

[71] For example, a bureaucrat is hedging or offsetting risks of exposure against incompetence or violation of regulations by hiding or shielding behind authority of public office.

1989). The principal-agent relations formulation deals with the problem of motivating the "agent" to act or efficiently perform a duty on behalf of the "principal". The problem is conceived in a setting where information asymmetry, uncertainty and risk are prominent, and where the agent, in order to perform certain acts (duties) that are useful to the principal, needs to engage in extensive search of information and incurs undisclosed costs.

Various methods of providing incentives for the agent to act in the desired way are widely discussed in the literature, e.g. employment contracts (Prendergast, 1999); (Milgrom, Paul and John Roberts, 1992), non-financial compensation (Green, J. R. and N. L. Stokey, 1983); team production (Alchian, Armen A. and Harold Demsetz, 1972); payment-by-results (PBR) schemes; etc. These are incentive provision methods to reconcile the principal-agent interests and relations for a private sector operator.

In the private sector, there is a gain to be made by the company which owns information in withholding it from competitors and "buying" the agent (the contract employee of the company with access to company information) to be a part of the company's business strategy. This approach is pursued more vigorously in situations where the stakes are high: when information is critical to profit margins and where the company has a large share of the market asset value.

The problems are posited differently in government, however. Government is more in the nature of a monopoly and the operations and behaviors of the public system are structured differently from that of the private sector who gains by keeping trade secrets. A major interest of government is to produce and manage information effectively and efficiently. Transparency in government is the hallmark of its "trade", which is good governance. Both the company and government gain by the production of information, but unlike the company, government does not benefit, but probably loses, by not producing, withholding or not efficiently managing information.[72]

---

[72] Government may benefit from "certain secrets" such as defense secrets, in the protection of human rights or liberty rights, etc.

To begin with, pay incentives may not always work effectively and efficiently, if the probability of success in buying the services of the agent (holder of a public office) by an outside interest group remains high and statistically significant. The individual voter has,

$$(1/number of\ voters) x (value of\ public policy)$$

Share of the stake, and only,

$$\left[\frac{1}{number\ of\ voters} \right]$$

Of the votes, and this vote power may not count for much. However, information is critical for the citizen, whose participation in government is dependent on government transparency. The interest of the citizen, and, therefore, that of government is ranged against that of the "agent" (or holder of public office), who has access to privileged information and the capacity to withhold and use that information to profit. The agent (or bureaucracy) is empowered by law to determine entry and prices of regulated industry, and uses his position as regulator to prosper (Peltzman, 1976); and (Stigler, 1971). It is also worth noting that the agent is in the best position to strategize and hedge against exposure or disclosure of his/her unlawful act by colluding with coworkers, or other officers of government.

Lack of transparency means, in this case, government (the voter or principal), which relies on the agent and the bureaucracy for accurate information does not get it. The principal is also constrained by the limited options available to induce transparency in government. Niskanen (Niskanen, 1971) notes that public reputation, patronage, and power are among the factors motivating correct behavior of the bureaucrat. But others question the validity of this behavioral assumption, against overwhelming evidence of unresponsiveness, invasion of privacy, excessive red-tapes, and corruption in government. To this group of analysts more credence is to be accorded to the utilitarian motives of utility and profit maximization under uncertainty. Even then, the way pecuniary incentives work varies. The balanced application of the "carrot" and "stick" method in the design of incentives is complicated and requires fine-tuning skills in government which may not be there (Deming, 1986). The government pay incentive is always offset by a higher pay offer to the agent by outside interest groups. The "exit" mechanism is not a viable option because the agent who quits (is expelled from office) will be replaced by another who will do the same, i.e. sell information for personal gains to interest groups (Stiglitz, 1989; (Hirschman, 1970).[73] "Voice" as the option for the principal (voter or government) implies among other things maintaining continued relationship with the agent, greater vigilance, intervention, oversight and increased cost, e.g. training the agent, greater supervision costs, more research and structuring new PBR incentive systems. In other words, improved transparency and accountability in government can come about through increased costs to society, i.e. legislation, increased budgetary appropriation and expanded bureaucratization. Cooperation should also be sought to work closely with operators in Box C (Figure 2) to inculcate desirable values and value systems in society.

Box 9: Variations on the Theme of "Good Governance"

In May 2008, it was reported widely[74] that the Ethiopian Prime Minister, Ato Melese Zenawi, held discussions with members of the business community and Ethiopian Chambers of Commerce and Sectoral Associations (ECCSA). The occasion was used by the meeting to request the prime Minister to return the office building of the Chamber, which was nationalized by the Derg some 32 years ago. The PM made a decision on the spot to return the building, and the Chamber issued congratulations to its members and thanked the PM for his prompt response to their request. How do you analyze this in the framework of "good governance" and the theory of private property development?

To see what is involved here, let us begin by showing what would happen if the US president ordered the driver of an illegally parked car on the road to clear. First, the fellow who parked the car will tell the President that it is none of his business and will refuse to follow the orders of the President. Second, the traffic police department will lodge an accusation in the courts against the President for impersonating a police officer (an illegal act). Thirdly, the (private) media will have a

---

[73] The probability of loss associated with risk-taking (resulting from exposure and punishment) is always offset by the greater probability of success to profit from authority in public office. Note too that the agent made to account for oversight looses: once the agent left office, she/he will have no value to private interests; except perhaps through "connection intermediation", which implies increased transaction costs.

[74] The Prime Minister's "decision" to return a building to the ECCSA, made in the course of their meeting with the PM of 12 May 2008, has been reported by: *Admas* of Ginbot 9, 2000 (17 May 2008); *Capital* of 18 May 2008; *Addis Zemen* of 5 Ginbot 2000 (13 May 2008); and *The Ethiopian Herald* of Tuesday, 13 May 2008 (Vol. LXIV No. 210.

field-day over the "scandal"; and fourthly, the President's party will ask the president and officers of government involved in any cover-up concerning the case to resign immediately. It would be fair to say the USA president will never do what we are supposing here – he cannot be that ignorant of the basic principles of administration and would never have become President of a modern state if he were capable of making this misjudgment.

Of course, PM Melese is not a President of the U.S.A., he is a PM of Ethiopia, where property right legislation, the bureaucracy and the institutional mechanisms and procedures for effective protection of property rights can at best be described presently as works in progress (if they can be described that way). It is difficult to ascertain whether or not this progress is being made on the basis of clear role assignments and legally correct procedures. One thing we know for sure is that the Derg nationalized private property by legislation and through the establishment of a Ministry of National Resources Development as the government receiver.

The congratulations and thanks from the Chamber are also a cause for worry. How do the Chamber people proceed to implement the "decision" of the PM to return the building to the Chamber? Imagine for a moment yourself in the capacity of the head of the bureaucracy in charge of public or collective property (if there is one) and faced with a delegation from the Chamber asking you to implement the decision of the PM. Would you act as the man who parked his car illegally did, and tell the Chamber people that you work for the bureaucracy and according to rules and procedures and that you are not an employee of the PM? Will you tell the Chamber people that you do not receive orders from the PM or anybody else through ETV, Radio Fana or government papers and inform them of the bureaucratic channels you are supposed to follow?

It is clear that denationalization cannot be done by the PM on a case by case basis, and the Chamber people would have done better for themselves had they asked the PM for a *reform* rather than for the *return* of property, which would have made the legal return of the property possible. They must understand that the PM cannot verify whether a particular property belonged to them or not in the first place without consulting his bureaucracy and without creating the bureaucracy by law if it did not exist. The PM cannot appoint himself as Minister of a denationalization program, without due parliamentary process and also because he cannot perform that function, while holding the PM office at the same time (*conflict of interest*).

If each succeeding political party begins its reign by destroying the bureaucracy of the people and ruling party before it, then it is impossible to foresee a situation whereby the accumulation process and private property development become possible in a sustainable way. The decision of the courts and the actions of government emanate, not from the constitution, the law and democratic governmental assignment of duties and responsibilities, but from the power and other claims of the rulers of the land.

Lacking in legitimacy and capacity in government, and non-differentiation between "ruling political party" and "government" are among the visible manifestations of "poor or bad governance" in Africa today.

The behavior of the PM and the ECCSA officials are described by the Amharic saying "teyayizo wode gedel", translation: "to join hands and trip over the cliff and fall to certain death in the ravine below".

5. Concluding Remark

The solution to the fundamental economic problem: resource scarcity and competition over scarce resources lies in the establishment of good-governance government everywhere in the world. With this great feat accomplished, it all means that the destruction of economy and society caused by man is at last under control. It means that man and planet Earth can still be destroyed by, for example, the earth moving off its orbit through changes in gravitational fields, or by some cosmic upheavals. Such occurrences are clearly beyond the control of man.

However, the containment of human destructiveness through establishment of good-governance government everywhere (this is the equivalent of a global government and global citizenship for all) makes it possible to unleash human creativity: the ability of man to invent and discover new things and new ways of doing things (private property development!), and this human creativity has no bounds. Who knows, mankind will then be able to traverse time and space and have a permanent existence in the limitless or boundless space.

Global good-governance government as a manmade idea changes all the time and is subject to continuous revision and adjustment by the will, decision and actions of man. G^4 is not in conflict with religion and belief systems in general. It accommodates and in fact welcomes all religions, beliefs and occult practices so long as they confine themselves to preparing the individual for life after death and contribute to the development of ethics and morality.[75] G^4 has no claim over divinity, and that way G^4 shows the true worth of religion is to be measured not by the body-bags produced but the number of lives saved.

---

[75] In *Dekike Estifanos* (cited earlier as work translated from *Geez*), Getachew Haile notes that Aba Estifanos and followers accused Zera Yakob the king for not confining himself to his reign of the earthly domain and for meddling in church affairs, which was their business. If Ethiopians seek the separation of religion and state, it is partly because the debate was concluded in the 14th century (although not necessarily in favour of the secularists at that time). It was as a result of these antecedents that Emperor Haile-Selassie developed the dictum: *Haimanot yegil new, ager gin yegara new.* Translated into English it means: "Religion is a private experience of the individual, but the country belongs to us all."

References

Alchian, Armen A. and Harold Demsetz. (1972). "Production, Information Costs and Economic Organization". *American Economic Review 62(5):777-795* .

Collier, P. (2007). *The Bottom Billion: Why the Poorest Countries Are Failing and What Can Be Done About It.* Oxford: Oxford University Press.

Deming, W. E. (1986). *Out of the Crisis.* MIT   Press.

Green, J. R. and N. L. Stokey. (1983). "A Comparison of Tournaments and Contracts". *Journal of Political Economy 91:349-364* .

Hirschman, A. O. (1970). *Exit, Voice, and Loyalty: Responses to Decline in Firms, Organizations and States.* Cambridge: Harvard University Press.

Milgrom, Paul and John Roberts. (1992). *Economics, Organization and Management.* London: Prentice-Hall.

Mulat, T. (1993). "Trends in Government Finance". *Ethiopian Journal of Economics* 1(2):73-100

Niskanen, W. J. (1971). *Bureaucracy and Representative Government.* Chicago: Aldine.

Peltzman, S. (1976). "Towards a More General Theory of Regulation". *Journal of Law and Economics* (August) .

Prendergast, C. (1999). "The Provision of Incentives in Firms". *Journal of Economic Literature* 37(March):7-63 .

Stigler, G. J. (1971). "The Theory of Economic Regulation". *Bell Journal of Economics and Management Science* 2:3-21 .

Stiglitz, J. E. (1989). "Principal and Agent". In J. Eatwell, M. Milgate, & P. Newman (Eds.), *The New Pelgrave. Allocation, Information and Markets.* New York: W.W. Norton.

Index

Index

E

economic rationale, 7
employment contracts, 85
entrepreneurial coordination, 23, 30
entrepreneurial coordinator, 2, 32
entrepreneurs, 47
establishment legislation, 28
ethical behavior, 28
Ethiopian Human Rights Council, 25
ethnocracies, 18
exit mechanism, 87
externalities, 73

F

failed-economies, iv
feudalist exploiter, 1
Firms, 29
flexible, 33
food-aid threshold, 42, 49
Foreign direct investment, 18,, 35, 48
foundation, 78
fraudulent trade, 44
free media, 77
freedom of thought, 66
Freedoms, 82

G

Geez, 16
the Geez cultural heritage, 64
Germans, 38
globalization process, 82
gospel, 54
government subsidy, 33
greatest happiness principle, 66

H

hedonistic utilitarianism, 66
heuristic calculations, 2
hibernate, 51
honest signals, 14
human creativity, 66
human rights, 32, 79

I

ideology, 52
incentives, 85
Inclusiveness, 83
incontrovertible evidence, 54
incrementa changes, 58
Individual Rational Responses, 46
individualism, 66
industrial relocations, 53
information asymmetry, 12
information costs, 6
institutional reform, 29
intellectual property rights, 69
intent, 12
interest groups, 44

J

Japanese, 38
job screening, 17
joker, 58

K

Kitchen Cabinet, 22

L

Law, 68
legal framework, 29
Liberties, 82
liberty-rights, 79
licenses, 78
long run changes, 4
long-distance education programs,
 19

M

M- and H- modes, 1
malicious intent, 35
management, 28, 29
manmade religion, 52
marginal cost prices, 2
Market Behavior, 29

Index

www.ingramcontent.com/pod-product-compliance
Lightning Source LLC
Chambersburg PA
CBHW031246280526
45784CB00004B/1746